CYBER CRIME IN INDIA

TRENDS, CHALLENGES, AND SOLUTIONS

RAHUL PANDIT

Copyright © Rahul Pandit
All Rights Reserved.

This book has been self-published with all reasonable efforts taken to make the material error-free by the author. No part of this book shall be used, reproduced in any manner whatsoever without written permission from the author, except in the case of brief quotations embodied in critical articles and reviews.

The Author of this book is solely responsible and liable for its content including but not limited to the views, representations, descriptions, statements, information, opinions and references ["Content"]. The Content of this book shall not constitute or be construed or deemed to reflect the opinion or expression of the Publisher or Editor. Neither the Publisher nor Editor endorse or approve the Content of this book or guarantee the reliability, accuracy or completeness of the Content published herein and do not make any representations or warranties of any kind, express or implied, including but not limited to the implied warranties of merchantability, fitness for a particular purpose. The Publisher and Editor shall not be liable whatsoever for any errors, omissions, whether such errors or omissions result from negligence, accident, or any other cause or claims for loss or damages of any kind, including without limitation, indirect or consequential loss or damage arising out of use, inability to use, or about the reliability, accuracy or sufficiency of the information contained in this book.

Made with ❤ on the Notion Press Platform
www.notionpress.com

Contents

About Author — v

Preface — vii

Acknowledgements — ix

Introduction to Cyber Crime in India: Trends and Methods — xi

1. The Digital Landscape Of India — 1

2. Common Types Of Cyber Crimes In India — 15

3. Methods And Techniques Used By Cyber Criminals — 29

4. Legal Framework For Cyber Crime In India — 37

5. Investigating Cyber Crimes In India — 48

6. Cyber Security Strategies And Solutions — 57

7. Emerging Trends In Cyber Crime — 67

8. The Future Of Cyber Crime In India — 78

Common Cyber Frauds: Modus Operandi and Prevention — 89

Resources for Reporting Cyber Crimes — 141

Glossary of Terms — 145

About Author

Rahul Pandit is an accomplished IT Consultant and Technology Specialist with extensive experience in leading innovative projects, particularly in E-Governance. As the CEO and Lead Consultant at Ideogram Technology Solutions Pvt Limited, Rahul has spearheaded a wide range of technology initiatives, including key e-governance projects for government departments and Jammu and Kashmir Police. Additionally, as an IT Consultant for Jammu Smart City, he has been instrumental in implementing Smart Governance solutions to enhance urban management. Rahul also serves as a Visiting Faculty at Sher-i-Kashmir Police Academy, where he has delivered lectures on Cybercrimes over the years.

The book "**Cyber Crime in India**" delves into the complex world of cybercrime in India, exploring its rapid evolution, the increasing sophistication of cyber attacks, and the legal frameworks developed to combat these threats. Through detailed case studies, the book illustrates the real-world impacts of cybercrime on individuals, businesses, and government entities. It discusses various types of cybercrimes such as identity theft, financial frauds, and cyber terrorism, providing insights into the methods used by cybercriminals and the preventive measures that can be adopted. Rahul's expertise in technology and cyber security brings a unique depth to the analysis, making this book an essential resource for anyone interested in understanding and combating cybercrime in India.

Preface

In today's rapidly digitizing world, cyber crime has emerged as one of the most pressing challenges for nations, businesses, and individuals alike. The digital revolution, while opening doors to tremendous opportunities, has also created new avenues for malicious actors to exploit vulnerabilities, disrupt systems, and compromise data. India, as a nation that is undergoing one of the most significant digital transformations, finds itself at the forefront of this battle against cyber crime.

As internet penetration deepens and more sectors of the economy become digital-first, the complexity and sophistication of cyber threats are evolving at an alarming rate. From financial fraud and identity theft to state-sponsored cyber espionage and ransomware attacks, India faces a wide range of cyber threats that demand immediate and innovative solutions. The impact of these crimes is felt not just in economic terms but also in the erosion of trust in digital systems and the significant socio-economic consequences for citizens and businesses alike.

Cyber Crime in India: Trends, Challenges, and Solutions aims to address the growing concerns surrounding cyber security in India by providing a comprehensive analysis of the evolving landscape of cyber threats, the techniques used by cyber criminals, and the strategies needed to combat these threats. This book explores the various types of cyber crimes affecting India today, the methods cyber criminals use to perpetrate these crimes, and the critical role that legal frameworks, forensics, and public-private partnerships play in fighting back.

The chapters in this book cover everything from identity theft and financial fraud to cutting-edge technologies like quantum computing and artificial intelligence, which will shape the future of both cyber crime and cyber defense. In addition, the book delves into India's role in the global fight against cyber crime, highlighting the country's contributions to international cyber security initiatives and outlining a roadmap for a secure digital future.

This book is intended for policymakers, business leaders, law enforcement professionals, and citizens who want to better understand the complex world of cyber crime and what can be done to build a resilient cyber ecosystem in India. By raising awareness, fostering collaboration, and encouraging proactive measures, it is my hope that this book will contribute to a safer and more secure digital environment for all.

I invite you to explore **Cyber Crime in India: Trends, Challenges, and Solutions**, a journey into the future of digital security and the collective effort needed to combat the ever-growing threat of cyber crime.

Rahul Pandit

Acknowledgements

I would like to extend my heartfelt gratitude to the officers of the Jammu & Kashmir Police for their invaluable support and guidance throughout the development of this book. Their insights, expertise, and dedication have not only enriched my understanding of cyber crime but also provided a deeper perspective on the unique challenges faced in this domain.

The officers' willingness to share their experiences, discuss ongoing challenges, and provide real-world examples has been instrumental in enhancing the quality and depth of this work. Their knowledge of the complexities involved in investigating, preventing, and prosecuting cyber crimes has added a practical dimension to the theoretical and legal frameworks explored in this book. I am especially grateful for the time they dedicated to sharing their perspectives on cyber security and law enforcement, often going beyond their official duties to ensure that I had a comprehensive understanding of the issues.

The Jammu & Kashmir Police's commitment to safeguarding the public in the face of evolving cyber threats is both inspiring and commendable. Their contributions have not only influenced this book but have also deepened my respect for the challenging and critical work they perform daily.

To the officers of the Jammu & Kashmir Police, thank you for your support, mentorship, and encouragement. This book would not have been possible without your insights, and I am deeply grateful for the knowledge and experience you have shared with me.

Introduction To Cyber Crime In India: Trends And Methods

Cyber crime has rapidly evolved into one of the most significant threats of the 21st century, impacting individuals, businesses, and governments alike. In a digitally connected world, cyber criminals are exploiting technological advancements for illegal activities, often outpacing the capacity of law enforcement and legislative bodies to counter these crimes effectively. In India, the digital revolution has opened new avenues for growth and development but has also exposed the country to a range of cyber threats. This chapter introduces the reader to the concept of cyber crime, its scope, its historical evolution in India, and why it is a pressing issue today.

What is Cyber Crime?

Cyber crime refers to illegal activities where a computer or a networked device, such as a mobile phone, is used as a tool or a target. Unlike traditional crimes that often involve physical actions, cyber crimes are typically committed through digital means, making detection and prosecution more complex. Cyber crimes can range from minor offenses, such as online harassment, to major infractions, such as state-sponsored hacking or cyber terrorism.

Categories of Cyber Crime

Cyber crimes can be broadly classified into two main categories:

- **Crimes that target computer systems or networks:** These include offenses where the computer is the primary target of the crime, such as hacking, malware attacks, ransomware, or denial-of-service (DoS) attacks.

The objective here is usually to gain unauthorized access to systems or to disable services.

- **Crimes that use computers as tools to commit other offenses**: In this category, computers are used as a medium to perpetrate crimes like identity theft, financial fraud, or cyberstalking. Here, the computer is not the target but a means to execute traditional crimes in a more sophisticated, digital form.

The Expanding Scope of Cyber Crime

As technology continues to evolve, so too does the scope of cyber crime. With the rise of social media, mobile applications, cloud computing, and cryptocurrency, cyber criminals have found new ways to exploit vulnerabilities. The proliferation of the Internet of Things (IoT) devices has expanded the attack surface, with hackers now able to target everything from smart appliances to vehicles.

Some of the common forms of cyber crime include:

- **Hacking**: Gaining unauthorized access to a computer system or network.
- **Phishing and Social Engineering**: Deceptive tactics used to trick individuals into revealing sensitive information.
- **Ransomware**: A type of malware that encrypts a victim's data, demanding payment for decryption.
- **Identity Theft**: Stealing personal information, such as credit card numbers, to commit fraud.
- **Cyber Espionage**: Unauthorized access to confidential information for economic, political, or military gain.

In India, the diversity of cyber crime is immense, affecting sectors such as banking, healthcare, education, and government. The increased use of mobile phones and the internet has led to a rise in crimes such as phishing, ransomware attacks, and financial frauds, making cyber security a top priority for the country.

Historical Context: Evolution of Cyber Crime in India

The digital transformation of India began in the late 1990s with the liberalization of its economy and the growth of its IT sector. Since then, India has witnessed an exponential rise in internet users, driven by affordable smartphones and cheaper data plans. However, this rapid digitization has also brought with it the rise of cyber crime. The evolution of cyber crime in India can be broken down into several phases:

The Early Days: 1990s to Early 2000s

The initial phase of cyber crime in India was marked by relatively simple attacks, often carried out by individuals or small groups of hackers. These early crimes typically involved defacement of websites, small-scale hacking, and online fraud. However, as internet usage increased, so did the complexity of the attacks.

- **IT Act, 2000**: To combat the growing threat of cyber crime, the Indian government introduced the Information Technology (IT) Act in 2000. The IT Act provided a legal framework to address issues such as hacking, unauthorized access to data, and cyber terrorism. However, given the nascent stage of internet development in India at the time, the Act was limited in scope.

Mid-2000s: Growth of E-Commerce and Online Banking

With the rise of e-commerce platforms like Flipkart and Snapdeal and the proliferation of online banking, the nature of cyber crime in India began to change. Hackers now targeted customer data, online transactions, and payment gateways.

- **Phishing Attacks on Banking Sector**: One of the most common cyber crimes during this period was phishing. Hackers would send emails impersonating banks or e-commerce platforms, tricking users into divulging their login credentials or credit card information. According to the Reserve Bank of India (RBI), phishing attacks accounted for a significant portion of online fraud cases during this period.

Late 2010s: The Rise of Mobile Internet and Digital India

By the late 2010s, India had emerged as one of the largest digital markets in the world, with over 500 million internet users. This period also saw the government's push for the Digital India initiative, which aimed to provide digital services to citizens and increase internet penetration in rural areas.

- **Mobile Banking and UPI Frauds**: The advent of mobile banking and the Unified Payments Interface (UPI) led to an increase in financial frauds. In 2019, UPI frauds accounted for a large percentage of cyber crimes reported to the National Cyber Crime Reporting Portal.
- **Aadhaar Data Breach**: One of the most notable cyber crimes during this period was the alleged Aadhaar data breach. In 2018, reports surfaced that a database containing the personal information of over 1 billion

Indians had been compromised. While the government initially denied the breach, the incident raised serious concerns about the security of India's digital infrastructure.

2020s and Beyond: The Age of AI, Ransomware, and Cyber Terrorism

In recent years, cyber crime in India has become more sophisticated, with attackers leveraging emerging technologies like artificial intelligence (AI) and machine learning (ML). Ransomware attacks have surged, and cyber terrorism has become a growing concern for national security.

- **Ransomware Attacks:** In 2020, several Indian businesses and government organizations were targeted by ransomware attacks. These attacks involved the encryption of critical data, with the attackers demanding a ransom (usually in cryptocurrency) for its release. For example, the WannaCry ransomware attack of 2017, which affected several Indian companies, was a wake-up call for the need for stronger cyber defenses.
- **Cyber Terrorism:** India has also become a target for cyber terrorism, with state-sponsored actors attempting to hack into critical infrastructure such as power grids, communication networks, and defense systems. In 2020, it was reported that a cyber attack originating from China had targeted Mumbai's power grid, leading to widespread blackouts.

Why Cyber Crime Matters
Impact on Individuals

Cyber crime has a profound impact on individuals, affecting their personal, financial, and emotional well-being. The rise of digital services means that almost every aspect of a person's life is now linked to the internet, making individuals more vulnerable to cyber attacks.

Identity Theft and Financial Fraud

One of the most common cyber crimes affecting individuals is identity theft. In this type of crime, cyber criminals steal personal information such as social security numbers, credit card details, or online banking credentials. Once they have this information, they can engage in fraudulent activities such as opening new bank accounts, taking out loans, or making unauthorized purchases.

- **Case Study: Phishing Attacks in India**: In 2019, the RBI reported that phishing attacks targeting Indian banks were on the rise. Hackers would send fake emails pretending to be from legitimate banks, tricking users into revealing their login credentials. According to RBI data, such attacks led to financial losses amounting to ₹615 crore (approximately $82 million) in that year alone.

Emotional and Psychological Impact

In addition to the financial consequences, cyber crime can have a severe emotional and psychological impact on victims. Individuals who fall prey to online harassment, cyberstalking, or blackmail often experience stress, anxiety, and depression.

- **Case Study: Cyberbullying and Harassment**: Cyberbullying has become a growing problem, particularly among teenagers. In 2020, a report by the

NGO Child Rights and You (CRY) highlighted that nearly 30% of Indian teenagers had experienced some form of online harassment. The anonymity provided by the internet often emboldens cyberbullies, making it difficult for victims to seek justice.

Impact on Businesses

The business sector, particularly small and medium enterprises (SMEs), has been hit hard by the rise in cyber crime. For companies, the consequences of a cyber attack can be devastating, with financial losses, reputational damage, and legal liabilities.

Ransomware Attacks and Downtime

Ransomware has emerged as one of the biggest threats to businesses in India. When a company falls victim to a ransomware attack, its data is encrypted, and the attackers demand a ransom in exchange for the decryption key. This can lead to significant downtime, resulting in lost revenue and operational inefficiencies.

- **Case Study: The WannaCry Attack in India**: In 2017, the WannaCry ransomware attack affected several Indian organizations, including banks, hospitals, and manufacturing companies. The ransomware encrypted critical data, demanding payment in cryptocurrency for its release. The attack caused widespread disruptions, with companies losing millions in revenue.

Corporate Espionage and Data Theft

In addition to ransomware, corporate espionage has become a growing concern for businesses. Hackers often target companies to steal sensitive information, such as trade secrets, product designs, or customer data. This information can be sold on the dark web or used by competitors to gain an advantage.

- **Case Study: Hacking of Indian Pharmaceutical Companies**: In 2021, it was reported that several Indian pharmaceutical companies, including those involved in developing COVID-19 vaccines, had been targeted by state-sponsored hackers. The attackers sought to steal intellectual property related to vaccine development, raising concerns about the security of India's biotech industry.

Impact on Governments

Cyber crime poses a significant threat to national security, particularly when critical infrastructure such as power grids, water supply systems, and communication networks are targeted. Governments around the world, including India, have recognized the need for robust cyber defenses to protect their digital assets.

Cyber Warfare and Espionage

In recent years, cyber warfare has emerged as a new battleground for state-sponsored actors. Countries are increasingly using cyber attacks to engage in espionage, sabotage, and disruption of critical services. These attacks are often carried out by state-sponsored hackers who operate with the backing of governments.

- **Case Study: Power Grid Attack in Mumbai**: In 2020, a cyber attack originating from China targeted Mumbai's power grid, leading to widespread blackouts in the city. The attack was seen as an act of cyber warfare, aimed at disrupting India's critical infrastructure. The incident highlighted the vulnerabilities of India's power sector and the need for stronger cyber security measures.

Socio-Economic Consequences in India

Economic Losses

Cyber crime has a significant economic impact on India, with both direct and indirect costs. According to a study by cybersecurity firm McAfee, cyber crime costs the global economy over $600 billion annually. In India, the financial impact of cyber crime is estimated to be in the billions of dollars, affecting industries such as banking, healthcare, and telecommunications.

- **Direct Financial Losses**: The financial losses associated with cyber crime are often immediate and tangible. For example, a company that falls victim to a ransomware attack may have to pay a ransom to regain access to its data. In some cases, the ransom demanded can run into millions of rupees.
- **Indirect Costs**: In addition to direct financial losses, cyber crime also results in indirect costs such as loss of productivity, reputational damage, and legal fees. Companies that suffer data breaches may lose customers and face regulatory fines, further compounding their financial losses.

Impact on Digital Transformation

The Indian government has made significant strides in promoting digital transformation through initiatives such as Digital India and Smart Cities. However, the rise of cyber crime poses a threat to these efforts, as citizens and businesses may become hesitant to adopt digital services due to concerns about security and privacy.

- **Aadhaar and Public Trust**: The Aadhaar data breach highlighted the potential risks associated with large-scale digital initiatives. While Aadhaar was designed to streamline government services and reduce fraud, the breach raised concerns about the security of citizens' personal information. As a result, public trust in the system was eroded, with many questioning the government's ability to protect sensitive data.

Government Response and Cyber Security Initiatives
Recognizing the growing threat of cyber crime, the Indian government has taken several steps to strengthen its cyber security infrastructure. These include the establishment of the Indian Computer Emergency Response Team (CERT-In), the launch of the National Cyber Security Policy (NCSP), and the introduction of data protection laws.

- **CERT-In**: The Indian Computer Emergency Response Team (CERT-In) plays a crucial role in monitoring and responding to cyber threats in India. As the country's nodal agency for cyber security, CERT-In coordinates efforts between government agencies, private sector companies, and law enforcement to address cyber security incidents.
- **National Cyber Security Policy (NCSP)**: Launched in 2013, the NCSP provides a framework for securing India's digital infrastructure. The policy emphasizes the need for public-private partnerships, international cooperation, and capacity building to combat cyber crime effectively.

Key takeaways

The rise of cyber crime in India is a direct consequence of the country's rapid digital transformation. While the internet has brought about significant benefits in terms of connectivity and convenience, it has also created new vulnerabilities that cyber criminals are eager to exploit. The impact of cyber crime is far-reaching, affecting individuals, businesses, and governments alike.

As India continues on its path toward becoming a digital economy, the need for robust cyber security measures has never been more urgent. By strengthening its legal frameworks, investing in cyber security infrastructure, and promoting digital literacy, India can mitigate the risks posed by cyber crime and build a more secure digital future for its citizens.

CHAPTER I

The Digital Landscape of India

India is in the midst of a digital revolution. Over the past decade, the country has emerged as one of the largest digital markets in the world, driven by widespread internet access and mobile penetration. The government's "Digital India" initiative has accelerated this transformation, aiming to leverage technology to improve governance, provide digital services, and promote economic growth. However, as the country embraces digitalization, it also faces an increasing number of cyber threats. This chapter explores the growth of internet usage, mobile penetration, and the rise of digital platforms in India, along with the associated challenges and vulnerabilities in the context of cyber security.

Growth of Internet Usage and Mobile Penetration

India has witnessed an exponential growth in internet usage over the past two decades. From being a country with limited connectivity in the early 2000s, India has become the second-largest internet market in the world, with over 700 million active internet users as of 2023. This growth has been fueled by several factors, including affordable smartphones, low-cost data plans, and government initiatives to improve digital infrastructure.

Mobile Penetration: The Driver of Internet Growth

Mobile phones have been the primary driver of internet growth in India. According to data from the Telecom Regulatory Authority of India (TRAI), there are over 1.2 billion mobile phone users in the country, with nearly 75% of them using smartphones. This widespread access to mobile phones has enabled millions of Indians, including those in rural areas, to access the internet for the first time.

- **Affordable Smartphones:** The availability of low-cost smartphones, particularly from manufacturers such as Xiaomi, Samsung, and Oppo, has made it possible for even low-income households to own a smartphone. This has played a critical role in increasing mobile internet penetration, with the number of smartphone users crossing 600 million in 2023.
- **Cheap Data Plans:** India is known for having some of the lowest data costs in the world. The entry of Reliance Jio in 2016 revolutionized the telecom market by offering free voice calls and extremely affordable data plans. As a result, data consumption in India skyrocketed, with the average Indian consuming 11 GB of data per month in 2022, compared to just 700 MB in 2014.
- **Rural Connectivity:** Mobile phones have also been instrumental in bridging the urban-rural digital divide. While urban areas were the first to benefit from internet access, rural India has seen a surge in connectivity in recent years. As of 2023, over 300 million rural Indians had access to the internet, with mobile phones being the predominant mode of access.

Government Initiatives to Boost Internet Access

The Indian government has played a crucial role in expanding internet access across the country. Several key initiatives have been launched to improve digital infrastructure and promote digital inclusion:

- **BharatNet Project:** Launched in 2011, BharatNet aims to provide high-speed broadband connectivity to all 250,000 Gram Panchayats (village councils) across India. The project seeks to bridge the digital divide between urban and rural areas by providing last-mile connectivity through optical fiber networks.
- **Digital India Programme:** Launched in 2015, the Digital India programme aims to transform India into a digitally empowered society and knowledge economy. The programme focuses on three key areas: providing digital infrastructure as a utility to every citizen, delivering government services digitally, and fostering digital literacy.

Impact of Internet Growth on Various Sectors

The rapid growth of internet usage has had a profound impact on various sectors of the Indian economy. Key industries such as e-commerce, banking, education, and healthcare have been transformed by the rise of digital platforms and services.

- **E-commerce:** India's e-commerce sector has experienced tremendous growth, with companies such as Flipkart, Amazon, and Paytm leading the charge. The number of online shoppers in India reached 150 million in 2023, driven by increasing internet penetration, the rise of digital payment systems, and the growing middle class.
- **Banking and Finance:** The financial sector has also undergone significant digital transformation, with mobile banking, digital wallets, and the Unified Payments Interface (UPI) becoming popular methods of transaction. As of 2022, UPI accounted for over 60%

of digital payments in India, with over 6 billion transactions processed each month.

- **Education:** The internet has revolutionized the education sector, particularly during the COVID-19 pandemic. The adoption of online learning platforms such as BYJU'S, Unacademy, and Vedantu has allowed students to access educational content from the comfort of their homes. Additionally, government initiatives like the National Digital Library of India have made educational resources more accessible.

- **Healthcare:** Telemedicine and digital health platforms have become increasingly popular in India. Mobile apps such as Practo, 1mg, and Medlife have made it easier for patients to consult with doctors, order medicines, and access healthcare services remotely. The government's Ayushman Bharat Digital Mission, launched in 2021, aims to create a digital health ecosystem that provides seamless access to healthcare services for all citizens.

Digital India: Opportunities and Challenges

The Digital India initiative, launched by the Indian government in 2015, is one of the most ambitious projects aimed at transforming the country into a digitally empowered society. The programme has opened up numerous opportunities for economic growth, governance, and citizen engagement. However, it has also created several challenges, particularly in the areas of cyber security and data protection.

Opportunities Created by Digital India

Digital India has unlocked several opportunities for growth and innovation across various sectors. By leveraging technology, the initiative seeks to improve governance, boost entrepreneurship, and enhance service delivery.

- **E-Governance:** One of the core objectives of Digital India is to enhance the delivery of government services through digital platforms. Initiatives such as the UMANG app (Unified Mobile Application for New-age Governance), DigiLocker, and the Government e-Marketplace (GeM) have made it easier for citizens to access services such as filing taxes, applying for government schemes, and storing important documents digitally.

- **Digital Payments:** The push for digital payments has been a key focus of Digital India. The demonetization of 2016, which rendered 86% of the country's currency notes invalid overnight, served as a catalyst for the adoption of digital payment methods. UPI, digital wallets, and mobile banking have since become mainstream, with the volume of digital transactions growing by over 500% between 2017 and 2022.

- **Startups and Entrepreneurship:** The digital ecosystem in India has created fertile ground for startups and entrepreneurship. With over 90,000 registered startups as of 2023, India is now home to the third-largest startup ecosystem in the world. Technology-driven startups in sectors such as fintech, edtech, healthtech, and agritech have emerged as key contributors to the country's economic growth.

- **Digital Literacy:** Digital India has also prioritized digital literacy as a means of empowering citizens. The Pradhan Mantri Gramin Digital Saksharta Abhiyan (PMGDISHA) aims to provide digital literacy to 60 million rural households, helping individuals develop the skills necessary to use digital platforms and services effectively.

Challenges Faced by Digital India

While Digital India has created numerous opportunities, it has also brought several challenges that need to be addressed to ensure the initiative's long-term success.

- **Cyber Security Threats:** One of the most pressing challenges of Digital India is the rise in cyber security threats. As more services move online and the country's digital footprint expands, the risk of cyber attacks, data breaches, and financial frauds has increased significantly. India has witnessed a surge in cyber crime incidents, ranging from phishing attacks and ransomware to hacking of government websites and critical infrastructure.
- **Data Privacy and Protection:** The rapid digitalization of services has raised concerns about the privacy and security of citizens' personal data. The lack of a comprehensive data protection framework has left many individuals vulnerable to data breaches and misuse of personal information. While the Personal Data Protection Bill was introduced in 2019, it has faced delays in its implementation, leaving gaps in the legal framework for data protection.
- **Digital Divide:** Despite the progress made in expanding internet access, there remains a significant digital divide between urban and rural areas, as well as between different socio-economic groups. While urban areas have benefited from high-speed internet access and a wide range of digital services, rural areas continue to face challenges such as poor connectivity, lack of digital literacy, and limited access to digital infrastructure.

- **Digital Infrastructure:** Ensuring the reliability and resilience of India's digital infrastructure is another key challenge. Frequent outages, low internet speeds, and inadequate network coverage in certain regions have hindered the seamless delivery of digital services. The government's BharatNet project aims to address these issues by providing broadband connectivity to rural areas, but progress has been slow, and many regions still remain underserved.

The Rise of Cyber Vulnerabilities

As India embraces digital technologies, the country has also become increasingly vulnerable to cyber threats. The widespread adoption of the internet, mobile devices, and digital payment systems has created a fertile environment for cyber criminals. From hacking and identity theft to ransomware and cyber espionage, the range and sophistication of cyber threats have grown rapidly.

Key Factors Contributing to Cyber Vulnerabilities

Several factors have contributed to the rise of cyber vulnerabilities in India, making individuals, businesses, and government entities more susceptible to attacks.

- **Increased Digital Footprint:** With more services being offered online, the digital footprint of individuals and organizations has expanded significantly. This increase in online activity has made it easier for cyber criminals to exploit vulnerabilities and launch attacks. For example, the use of social media platforms, mobile apps, and e-commerce websites has created new avenues for phishing attacks, malware, and data breaches.
- **Lack of Cyber Security Awareness:** One of the biggest challenges in addressing cyber threats in India is the

lack of awareness among users about basic cyber hygiene. Many individuals and small businesses are unaware of the risks associated with weak passwords, unpatched software, or phishing scams. This lack of knowledge has made them easy targets for cyber criminals, who often use simple tactics to compromise systems.

- **Weak Cyber Security Infrastructure:** While large corporations and government agencies have invested in cyber security measures, many small and medium-sized enterprises (SMEs) lack the resources to implement robust security protocols. This has made them particularly vulnerable to cyber attacks, such as ransomware and malware infections. Additionally, critical infrastructure such as power grids, transportation systems, and healthcare networks remain vulnerable to cyber threats due to outdated security measures.
- **State-Sponsored Cyber Attacks:** In recent years, state-sponsored cyber attacks have emerged as a significant threat to national security. Countries such as China, Russia, and North Korea have been accused of launching cyber espionage campaigns aimed at stealing sensitive information, disrupting critical infrastructure, and influencing political processes. India has also been targeted by such attacks, with several incidents involving government agencies, defense systems, and financial institutions.

Common Types of Cyber Vulnerabilities in India

India faces a wide range of cyber vulnerabilities, many of which are a result of weak security practices, outdated technology, and a lack of regulatory oversight. Some of the most common types of cyber vulnerabilities in India include:

- **Phishing Attacks:** Phishing is one of the most prevalent forms of cyber attack in India. Cyber criminals use fake emails, websites, or messages to trick users into providing sensitive information, such as login credentials, credit card numbers, or personal data. Phishing attacks have become more sophisticated, with attackers often impersonating legitimate organizations or government agencies to gain the trust of their victims.
- **Ransomware:** Ransomware attacks have surged in recent years, with cyber criminals encrypting the victim's data and demanding a ransom in exchange for its release. In 2021, India ranked among the top three countries most affected by ransomware attacks, with sectors such as healthcare, finance, and education being particularly vulnerable. The WannaCry ransomware attack in 2017, which affected several Indian companies and government institutions, highlighted the growing threat of ransomware in the country.
- **Data Breaches:** Data breaches have become increasingly common in India, with cyber criminals targeting organizations to steal sensitive information such as customer data, financial records, and intellectual property. High-profile data breaches, such as the alleged Aadhaar data leak, have raised concerns about the security of personal information stored in government databases and private organizations.
- **IoT Vulnerabilities:** The rise of the Internet of Things (IoT) has introduced new vulnerabilities, as many IoT devices lack robust security features. Hackers can

exploit these weaknesses to gain access to connected devices, such as smart home systems, security cameras, and industrial control systems. In 2022, a report by Symantec revealed that India was one of the top targets for IoT-related cyber attacks.

Case Studies: Prominent Cyber Crimes in Recent Years

India has witnessed several high-profile cyber crimes in recent years, highlighting the growing threat of cyber attacks and the need for stronger security measures. These incidents have affected a wide range of sectors, from government institutions and financial services to healthcare and e-commerce. The following case studies illustrate the diversity and severity of cyber crimes in India.

Case Study 1: The Cosmos Bank Heist (2018)

In one of the most significant cyber crimes in Indian banking history, hackers siphoned off ₹94 crore from Cosmos Bank in Pune in 2018. The cyber criminals used a combination of malware and ATM withdrawals to carry out the attack, which involved cloning debit cards and making fraudulent transactions across multiple countries.

- **How the Attack Occurred:** The hackers gained access to the bank's ATM switch system, which allowed them to bypass the verification process and authorize fraudulent transactions. Over 12,000 transactions were made using cloned cards at ATMs in 28 countries, while a second wave of transactions targeted the bank's SWIFT system to transfer funds to a bank in Hong Kong.
- **Impact:** The incident highlighted vulnerabilities in the Indian banking system, particularly in terms of ATM

security and SWIFT transaction protocols. In response, the Reserve Bank of India (RBI) issued guidelines to improve the security of ATMs and strengthen cyber security measures in the banking sector.

Case Study 2: Aadhaar Data Breach (2018)

In 2018, the Aadhaar system, which is the world's largest biometric identification database, was allegedly breached, exposing the personal information of over 1 billion Indian citizens. The breach involved unauthorized access to the Aadhaar database, which contains sensitive information such as names, addresses, phone numbers, and biometric data.

- **How the Breach Occurred:** According to reports, a data broker was selling access to the Aadhaar database for as little as ₹500. The breach was facilitated through vulnerabilities in the system's API, which allowed unauthorized users to access personal information stored in the database.
- **Impact:** The breach raised serious concerns about the security of the Aadhaar system and the privacy of Indian citizens. It also led to widespread criticism of the government's handling of personal data and calls for stronger data protection laws. In response, the Unique Identification Authority of India (UIDAI) introduced additional security measures, including virtual ID and limited KYC, to protect users' data.

Case Study 3: The BigBasket Data Breach (2020)

In 2020, BigBasket, one of India's largest online grocery platforms, suffered a data breach that compromised the personal information of over 20 million customers. The breach included sensitive data such as names, email addresses, phone numbers, delivery addresses, and hashed passwords.

- **How the Breach Occurred:** The breach was detected by cybersecurity firm Cyble, which discovered that the stolen data was being sold on the dark web for around $40,000. The hackers exploited vulnerabilities in BigBasket's database to gain access to the user information.
- **Impact:** The incident raised concerns about the security of e-commerce platforms and the need for better protection of customer data. BigBasket was forced to initiate an internal investigation and strengthen its security protocols to prevent future breaches.

Case Study 4: Paytm Mall Data Breach (2020)

In 2020, Paytm Mall, the e-commerce arm of digital payments giant Paytm, was reportedly targeted by a cyber attack that compromised the personal and financial data of millions of users. The breach was allegedly carried out by the hacker group "John Wick," which demanded a ransom in exchange for not releasing the stolen data.

- **How the Breach Occurred:** The hackers exploited vulnerabilities in Paytm Mall's database to gain access to sensitive user information, including payment details. The breach was detected when the hackers posted about their success on online forums, claiming to have compromised the platform's security.
- **Impact:** The breach raised concerns about the security of digital payment platforms and the protection of user data. While Paytm denied that any sensitive information

had been compromised, the incident highlighted the need for stronger security measures in the e-commerce and digital payments sector.

Case Study 5: Mumbai Power Grid Cyber Attack (2020)

In October 2020, Mumbai experienced a massive power outage that affected millions of residents and businesses. It was later revealed that the power outage was the result of a cyber attack, allegedly carried out by a Chinese state-sponsored hacker group. The attack targeted the operational technology systems of Mumbai's power grid, disrupting the distribution of electricity.

- **How the Attack Occurred:** The attackers used malware to infiltrate the systems controlling the power grid. The malware allowed them to manipulate the grid's operations, causing a cascading failure that resulted in the blackout. The attack was believed to be part of a broader cyber espionage campaign targeting India's critical infrastructure.
- **Impact:** The incident underscored the vulnerabilities of India's critical infrastructure to cyber attacks and the potential consequences for national security. It also highlighted the growing threat of state-sponsored cyber warfare and the need for robust defenses to protect critical systems such as power grids, water supply networks, and transportation systems.

Key takeaways from this Chapter

The digital landscape of India has evolved rapidly over the past decade, creating immense opportunities for growth and innovation across various sectors. The expansion of internet access, mobile penetration, and digital services has transformed the way individuals, businesses, and governments operate. However, this digital transformation has also given rise to new challenges, particularly in the realm of cyber security.

As India continues its journey toward becoming a digitally empowered society, it must address the growing cyber vulnerabilities that accompany this transformation. From phishing attacks and ransomware to data breaches and state-sponsored cyber espionage, the country faces a wide range of threats that require a coordinated and comprehensive response. Strengthening cyber security infrastructure, promoting cyber awareness, and implementing robust data protection laws will be crucial to safeguarding India's digital future.

This chapter has provided an overview of the digital landscape in India, highlighting both the opportunities and challenges that have emerged as the country embraces digital technologies. In the following chapters, we will delve deeper into specific types of cyber crimes, the methods used by cyber criminals, and the legal frameworks in place to combat these threats.

CHAPTER II

Common Types of Cyber Crimes in India

Cyber crimes in India have witnessed an alarming rise due to the expansion of the digital ecosystem. With the growth of internet usage, mobile penetration, and digital financial services, criminals are exploiting vulnerabilities to commit crimes ranging from identity theft to cyber terrorism. In this chapter, we delve into the various types of cyber crimes that are most prevalent in India, providing real-world examples and case studies to understand their impact on individuals, businesses, and the nation.

Identity Theft

Identity theft involves stealing someone's personal information, such as name, address, financial details, or even biometric data, and using it for fraudulent activities like opening bank accounts, making unauthorized transactions, or taking out loans.

Methods of Identity Theft

1. **Phishing** Phishing remains one of the most common techniques for identity theft in India. It typically involves sending fraudulent emails or text messages pretending to be from legitimate institutions such as banks, credit card companies, or government agencies. These messages aim to trick the recipient into providing sensitive information such as passwords, credit card details, or Aadhaar numbers.

- **Example: SBI Phishing Scam (2020):** In 2020, cyber criminals targeted State Bank of India (SBI) customers by sending fraudulent emails that appeared to be from the bank, asking them to click on a link to update their KYC (Know Your Customer) information. The link directed the victims to a fake website that resembled the official SBI website, where they were asked to input their credentials, which were then stolen by the attackers.

2. **Spoofing** Spoofing involves creating a fake version of a legitimate entity, such as an email address or website, to deceive the victim into revealing sensitive information. Spoofing can be used in conjunction with phishing attacks to make them more convincing.

   - **Example: Indian Tax Refund Scam (2018):** In this case, criminals sent emails that looked like they were from the Indian Income Tax Department, informing recipients that they were eligible for a tax refund. Victims were asked to provide their bank account details and personal information to receive the refund. Once they entered this information, it was used to drain their bank accounts .

3. **Social Engineering** Social engineering is a non-technical method where attackers manipulate individuals into giving away confidential information. This often involves building trust with the victim through impersonation.

   - **Example: Paytm Social Engineering Fraud (2020):** In 2020, fraudsters pretending to be Paytm customer service agents called victims, claiming there were issues with their accounts. The victims were asked to provide OTPs (One Time Passwords) or card details, which were then used to access their digital wallets and bank accounts .

Notable Cases of Identity Theft

1. **Aadhaar Data Breach (2018)** The Aadhaar data breach of 2018 remains one of the most significant incidents of identity theft in India. A journalist from *The Tribune* newspaper reported that sensitive details of over 1.2 billion Indians were being sold on WhatsApp for as little as ₹500. This included Aadhaar numbers, names, addresses, and mobile numbers. While the Unique Identification Authority of India (UIDAI) denied any breach, the incident raised serious concerns about the security of India's digital identity infrastructure .

2. **OLX Identity Fraud (2021)** In 2021, numerous users of OLX, an online marketplace, reported being defrauded after sharing their personal details with fake buyers and sellers. The fraudsters would ask the victims to share sensitive information like Aadhaar numbers and bank details, which were then used to commit various financial frauds. This scam targeted individuals across multiple cities in India .

Financial Frauds

Cyber financial frauds include unauthorized access to bank accounts, credit card fraud, and scams involving digital payment systems such as the Unified Payments Interface (UPI). As more Indians rely on digital transactions, these crimes have grown exponentially.

Common Types of Financial Frauds

1. **Credit/Debit Card Frauds** Cyber criminals often use stolen credit or debit card information to make unauthorized transactions. This information can be obtained through skimming devices, phishing, or data breaches from online platforms.

   - **Example: ATM Skimming in Kolkata (2019):** In 2019, a gang of Romanian nationals installed skimming devices on several ATMs across Kolkata. These devices recorded users' card information and PINs, which were then used to clone cards and withdraw money from victims' accounts. Over 70 people reported losses totaling more than ₹20 lakh in this scam .

2. **Online Banking Scams** Online banking scams involve tricking individuals into revealing their login credentials for online banking platforms. Cyber criminals may use phishing attacks, malware, or social engineering to gain access to bank accounts.

   - **Example: ICICI Bank Phishing Attack (2017):** Cyber criminals sent emails pretending to be from ICICI Bank, asking users to update their login credentials for security reasons. Once users entered their information on a fake website, the attackers used the stolen details to make fraudulent transactions .

3. **UPI-Related Frauds** The UPI system has made digital payments easy and accessible for millions of Indians,

but it has also become a target for fraudsters. UPI frauds often involve fake payment requests, phishing links, or fraudulent customer support calls.

- ○ **Example: UPI Fake Payment Request Scam (2021):** In this scam, fraudsters would send fake UPI payment requests to victims, posing as buyers on e-commerce platforms like OLX or Facebook Marketplace. Unsuspecting victims would approve the payment request, thinking they were receiving money, but instead, the money was debited from their accounts .

Notable Cases of Financial Frauds

1. **Cosmos Bank Cyber Heist (2018)** One of India's largest cyber financial frauds occurred at Cosmos Bank in Pune, where hackers stole ₹94 crore by accessing the bank's ATM switch system. The criminals created over 12,000 cloned debit cards and used them to withdraw money from ATMs in 28 countries. The attack also involved unauthorized SWIFT transactions. This high-profile case highlighted the vulnerabilities in India's banking infrastructure .

2. **Yes Bank Data Leak (2020)** In 2020, Yes Bank customers were targeted in a phishing campaign where fraudsters sent fake emails claiming to offer special loan schemes during the COVID-19 pandemic. Customers were asked to share their personal and financial information to avail these loans, which was then used for fraudulent activities .

Cyber Stalking and Harassment

Cyber stalking and harassment have emerged as serious issues, particularly for women and minors. These crimes involve the use of digital platforms to intimidate, threaten, or exploit individuals, often leading to emotional distress and psychological harm.

Methods of Cyber Stalking and Harassment

1. **Social Media Exploitation** Social media platforms have become common spaces for harassment. Cyber stalkers may create fake profiles, send threatening messages, or post defamatory content to harass their victims.

   - **Example: Instagram Harassment Case (2021):** A woman in Delhi filed a police complaint after receiving abusive messages and death threats from a fake Instagram account. The stalker had been targeting her for months, sending harassing messages, and posting defamatory comments on her pictures .

2. **Revenge Porn** Revenge porn involves sharing intimate photos or videos of someone without their consent, often as a form of retaliation after a relationship ends. This can lead to severe psychological trauma for the victim.

   - **Example: Delhi Revenge Porn Case (2019):** In 2019, a man was arrested in Delhi for posting private videos of his ex-girlfriend online after she ended their relationship. The victim reported the incident to the Cyber Cell, leading to the arrest of the perpetrator .

3. **Doxing** Doxing refers to the public release of an individual's personal information, such as their home address, phone number, or workplace, to intimidate or harass them.

   ○ **Example: Bangalore Cyber Harassment (2020):** In 2020, a woman was doxed by an anonymous online group that posted her personal details on social media. She received numerous threats and had to file a police report. The police tracked down the perpetrators, who were charged under the IT Act .

Legal Frameworks for Protection

India has established several laws to protect individuals from cyber stalking and harassment:

- **The IT Act, 2000:** The Information Technology Act criminalizes acts such as publishing obscene material online and sending threatening messages. Sections 66A and 67 deal with online harassment and privacy violations.
- **Indian Penal Code (IPC):** Section 354D of the IPC specifically addresses stalking, including online stalking, while Sections 499 and 500 cover defamation, both online and offline.

Notable Cases of Cyber Stalking and Harassment

1. **Air India Flight Attendant Harassment Case (2019)** In 2019, an Air India flight attendant reported being cyber stalked by a man who had been harassing her on social media for months. The stalker created multiple fake profiles and sent her abusive messages. The victim

filed a police complaint, leading to the arrest of the stalker under charges of cyber stalking and harassment .

2. **Bangalore Cyber Bullying Case (2021)** A 16-year-old girl in Bangalore became the target of a cyber bullying campaign on Facebook, where a group of boys posted derogatory comments about her appearance. She filed a complaint with the Cyber Cell, and the perpetrators were identified and charged under Sections 66A and 67 of the IT Act .

Cyber Terrorism

Cyber terrorism refers to attacks that target government infrastructure, critical services, or national security through digital means. These attacks are often state-sponsored or carried out by terrorist groups aiming to disrupt essential services or steal classified information.

Common Types of Cyber Terrorism

1. **Hacking Government Infrastructure** Cyber terrorists often target government databases, websites, and communication networks to steal sensitive information or sabotage critical operations. These attacks can cripple essential services, disrupt governance, and compromise national security.

   - **Example: Indian Space Research Organisation (ISRO) Hack (2019):** In 2019, ISRO's communication networks were reportedly targeted by a suspected cyber attack just days before the Chandrayaan-2 mission. Although no critical data was compromised, the incident raised concerns about the security of India's space research infrastructure .

2. **Denial of Service (DoS) Attacks** Denial of Service (DoS) attacks involve overwhelming a website or network with traffic, making it inaccessible to users. Cyber terrorists often use these attacks to disrupt government services, media organizations, or financial institutions.

   ◦ **Example: Pakistan's Cyber Attack on Indian Government Sites (2017):** In 2017, a group of Pakistani hackers launched a DoS attack on several Indian government websites, rendering them inaccessible for hours. This attack was part of a larger cyber terrorism campaign aimed at disrupting India's digital infrastructure .

National Security Threats

India's critical infrastructure, including power grids, transportation systems, and defense networks, remains vulnerable to cyber attacks by terrorist groups and hostile nations. These attacks can lead to catastrophic consequences, including the loss of life, economic damage, and geopolitical instability.

• **Example: Mumbai Power Grid Attack (2020):** In October 2020, Mumbai experienced a massive power outage that disrupted life in India's financial capital for hours. Later reports revealed that the outage was likely the result of a cyber attack carried out by Chinese hackers targeting India's power grid infrastructure .

Notable Cases of Cyber Terrorism

1. **Indian Defense Ministry Breach (2018)** In 2018, Chinese hackers reportedly gained unauthorized access to India's Ministry of Defense systems, stealing sensitive military data. This breach raised alarms about the vulnerability of India's defense networks to cyber espionage and state-sponsored attacks .

2. **Kerala Cyber Attack on Power Grid (2021)** In 2021, the Kerala State Electricity Board (KSEB) reported a cyber attack on its power grid infrastructure, which had the potential to cause widespread disruptions in electricity distribution. Investigations revealed that the attack was orchestrated by foreign actors, highlighting the increasing threat of cyber terrorism targeting critical infrastructure .

Child Exploitation and Cyberbullying

The exploitation of children on digital platforms has become a global problem, with cyber criminals using the internet to commit crimes such as child pornography, grooming, and cyberbullying. These crimes often go unnoticed and can have lasting psychological effects on young victims.

Common Forms of Child Exploitation and Cyberbullying

1. **Digital Child Pornography** Cyber criminals use the internet, particularly the dark web, to distribute and access child pornography. India has seen a surge in such cases as more children gain access to the internet through mobile phones and computers.

   - **Example: Hyderabad Child Pornography Ring (2020):** In 2020, the Hyderabad police arrested a group of individuals involved in creating and distributing child pornography on the dark web. The ring operated across several states, using social media platforms to lure victims and exploit them for illegal content .

2. **Cyberbullying** Cyberbullying involves using digital platforms to harass, threaten, or humiliate children and teenagers. Social media platforms and messaging apps are often used for this purpose, leading to emotional distress and even suicidal tendencies in some cases.

   ◦ **Example: Blue Whale Challenge (2017):** The Blue Whale Challenge, an online game that allegedly led participants through a series of dangerous tasks, including self-harm, was linked to several teenage suicides in India. Victims were bullied into completing life-threatening challenges, and the game became a nationwide concern .

Laws and Measures to Combat Child Exploitation and Cyberbullying

India has enacted several laws to protect children from online exploitation and bullying. These include:

- **The Protection of Children from Sexual Offences (POCSO) Act, 2012:** The POCSO Act criminalizes child pornography and online grooming, providing stringent penalties for offenders.
- **The IT Act, 2000:** Sections 67B of the IT Act deal specifically with the publication and transmission of sexually explicit content involving minors.

- **National Commission for Protection of Child Rights (NCPCR):** The NCPCR has launched initiatives to raise awareness about cyberbullying and online safety for children.

Notable Cases of Child Exploitation and Cyberbullying

1. **Mumbai Child Pornography Case (2019)** In 2019, a man from Mumbai was arrested for running a child pornography ring on WhatsApp and Telegram, where he shared explicit videos and images of minors. The case was uncovered by a joint operation between Indian law enforcement agencies and international child protection groups .

2. **Cyberbullying in Delhi School (2020)** In 2020, a group of students at a prominent Delhi school was involved in cyberbullying a classmate on a WhatsApp group. The victim, a 15-year-old girl, was subjected to harassment and derogatory comments, leading her to suffer from severe anxiety and depression. The case highlighted the need for schools to take proactive measures against cyberbullying .

Key takeaways from this Chapter

Cyber crime in India has reached alarming levels, affecting individuals, businesses, and even national security. From identity theft and financial fraud to cyber terrorism and child exploitation, the scope of these crimes is vast and growing. The examples and cases discussed in this chapter illustrate the severity and variety of cyber crimes in India, emphasizing the need for robust cyber security measures, legal frameworks, and public awareness campaigns.

As India continues to digitize its economy and society, the challenge of combating cyber crime will only become more complex. In the next chapter, we will examine the tools and techniques used by cyber criminals, as well as the steps that individuals, businesses, and governments can take to protect themselves in the digital age.

References used in this Chapter

1. **SBI phishing scam 2020** – Economic Times (https://economictimes.indiatimes.com/wealth/personal-finance-news/sbi-warns-customers-about-new-phishing-scam-targeting-bank-account-details/articleshow/77095382.cms?from=mdr)

2. **Cosmos Bank cyber heist** – Indian Express (https://indianexpress.com/article/cities/pune/rbi-fines-cosmos-bank-rs-2-crore-in-connection-with-cyber-heist-case-7322784/)

3. **Yes Bank phishing attack** – Times of India (https://timesofindia.indiatimes.com/business/india-business/phishing-attacks-on-banks-are-on-the-rise/articleshow/66685012.cms)

4. **Blue Whale Challenge and its impact** – The Hindu (https://www.thehindu.com/news/national/other-states/the-blue-whale-challenge-game-what-is-it-and-why-is-it-linked-to-suicides/article19475504.ece)

5. **Mumbai power grid cyber attack** – BBC (https://www.bbc.com/news/world-asia-india-56345591)

6. **Hyderabad child pornography case** – Hindustan Times (https://www.hindustantimes.com/india-news/hyderabad-man-arrested-for-allegedly-circulating-child-pornography/story-

pW4Z0EBfRglq6rOBr98LUN.html)
7. **ISRO hacking incident** – Times of India (https://timesofindia.indiatimes.com/india/isro-not-targeted-by-cyber-attack/articleshow/70394031.cms)

CHAPTER III

Methods and Techniques Used by Cyber Criminals

Cyber criminals employ a wide range of sophisticated methods and techniques to carry out illegal activities, exploiting vulnerabilities in technology and human behavior. These methods have evolved in complexity as technology has advanced, leading to an increase in the frequency and impact of cyber crimes. This chapter delves into some of the most common hacking techniques, including malware, ransomware, spyware, social engineering attacks, the role of the dark web, and how cryptocurrency facilitates illicit transactions. Real-world examples highlight the scale and impact of these cyber crimes, demonstrating why it is crucial for individuals, businesses, and governments to remain vigilant and adopt robust cybersecurity measures.

Hacking Techniques

Hacking techniques have evolved over time, becoming more complex and dangerous. Cyber criminals employ various forms of hacking to infiltrate systems, steal data, and disrupt services. The most common and damaging hacking techniques include **malware**, **ransomware**, and **spyware**, each with distinct characteristics and impacts.

Malware and Ransomware

Malware is a broad term used to describe any malicious software that is designed to harm, exploit, or take control of a computer system. It can include viruses, worms, trojans, and spyware. **Ransomware** is a specific type of malware that encrypts a victim's files and demands a ransom, usually in cryptocurrency, to unlock the data. The consequences of a ransomware attack can be devastating for individuals, businesses, and governments, resulting in lost data, financial damages, and reputational harm.

Example: WannaCry Ransomware Attack (2017)

The **WannaCry ransomware attack** was one of the most widespread and damaging cyber attacks in history, affecting over 300,000 computers in 150 countries. It exploited a vulnerability in the Microsoft Windows operating system, encrypting data and locking users out of their systems. Victims were asked to pay a ransom in Bitcoin to regain access to their files. The attack had significant repercussions in India, where multiple industries, including banking and transportation, were impacted. Globally, the National Health Service (NHS) in the UK was among the hardest hit, with operations disrupted in many hospitals.

Example: Petya Ransomware Attack (2017)

Following closely on the heels of WannaCry, the **Petya ransomware attack** targeted major corporations across the world, including those in India. Petya functioned similarly to WannaCry, encrypting the entire system, rendering it useless until a ransom was paid. The logistics, retail, and manufacturing sectors in India were particularly affected. Unlike WannaCry, Petya not only encrypted files but also overwrote the master boot record, making data recovery almost impossible even after paying the ransom.

Spyware and Adware

Spyware is designed to secretly monitor a user's activities, often with the goal of stealing sensitive information such as passwords, financial data, or personal communications. **Adware**, while not always as malicious as spyware, can flood a user's system with unwanted ads, often redirecting them to malicious websites where further attacks can occur.

Example: Pegasus Spyware Incident (2019)

In 2019, it was revealed that **Pegasus spyware**, developed by the Israeli firm NSO Group, had been used to target journalists, activists, and political figures in India, among other countries. The spyware infected devices through missed WhatsApp calls, giving attackers access to all communications, contacts, and files stored on the device. This incident raised significant concerns about privacy and surveillance, especially as Pegasus was used against individuals involved in sensitive political activities.

Social Engineering Attacks

Social engineering attacks exploit human psychology to trick individuals into revealing confidential information or performing actions that compromise security. These attacks are often more successful than purely technical attacks because they bypass technological defenses by targeting the weakest link in the security chain—humans. Common forms of social engineering attacks include **phishing, vishing, SMiShing, baiting**, and **quid pro quo attacks.**

Phishing, Vishing, and SMiShing

- **Phishing** is an attempt to steal sensitive information such as login credentials or financial details through emails or websites that appear legitimate.
- **Vishing** (voice phishing) uses phone calls to impersonate legitimate entities, such as banks or government agencies, to trick victims into sharing information.

- **SMiShing** is a form of phishing that targets victims via SMS text messages, often leading them to malicious websites or asking for sensitive information through deceptive links.

Example: Phishing Attack on ICICI Bank Customers (2019)

In 2019, phishing attacks targeting **ICICI Bank customers** gained traction. Fraudsters sent emails that mimicked the bank's official communication, directing victims to fake websites that captured their login credentials and led to unauthorized withdrawals from their accounts.

Example: Vishing Scam Targeting Aadhaar Holders (2020)

In 2020, **Aadhaar cardholders** were targeted in a vishing scam where criminals impersonated government officials and requested personal information under the pretense of updating Aadhaar details. Victims unknowingly provided one-time passwords (OTPs), leading to financial fraud.

Baiting and Quid Pro Quo Attacks

Baiting involves offering something enticing, such as free software or access to exclusive content, in exchange for sensitive information or downloading malware. **Quid pro quo** attacks involve offering a service or benefit in exchange for the victim's personal information, often under the guise of technical support.

Example: Baiting Attack on Mumbai University (2019)

In 2019, students at **Mumbai University** were targeted in a baiting attack where fraudsters offered free access to paid academic software. Students who downloaded the software unknowingly installed malware that harvested their credentials and personal information.

Dark Web: A Marketplace for Cyber Crime

The **dark web** is a hidden part of the internet that requires specialized software like **Tor** to access. It is often associated with illegal activities, providing anonymity and encryption that allow cyber criminals to operate in secrecy. The dark web serves as a marketplace for the sale of drugs, weapons, stolen data, hacking tools, and other illicit goods and services. The anonymity provided by cryptocurrency transactions on the dark web has made it a hub for cyber crime.

Accessing and Functioning of the Dark Web

The dark web operates through sophisticated encryption technologies that make it difficult for law enforcement to track users. Criminals create **hidden marketplaces** where goods and services are exchanged, often in return for cryptocurrency.

Example: AlphaBay Dark Web Marketplace Shutdown (2017)

AlphaBay, one of the largest dark web marketplaces, was taken down in a global law enforcement operation in 2017. AlphaBay facilitated the sale of illegal drugs, weapons, stolen data, and malware, and Indian users were reportedly involved in several transactions. Its shutdown dealt a major blow to dark web trading, but many similar platforms have since emerged.

Illegal Transactions: Drugs, Weapons, and Stolen Data

The dark web has become a hub for illegal transactions, including the sale of stolen credit card data, hacked accounts, drugs, weapons, and more. Cyber criminals frequently buy and sell these goods, often using cryptocurrency to avoid detection.

Example: Stolen Indian Credit Card Data on Dark Web (2019)

In 2019, it was reported that over **1.3 million Indian credit and debit card details** were being sold on the dark web for as little as $10 each. This data was likely obtained through phishing schemes, malware infections, and other hacking methods.

Cryptocurrency and Cyber Crime

Cryptocurrencies like **Bitcoin** and privacy-focused coins such as **Monero** have revolutionized online transactions by providing a decentralized, anonymous method for transferring value. Unfortunately, this anonymity also makes cryptocurrency the preferred method of payment for cyber criminals, especially in ransomware attacks, illegal purchases on the dark web, and other forms of cyber crime.

How Crypto is Used in Illicit Transactions

Cyber criminals use cryptocurrency to anonymize their financial transactions, making it difficult for law enforcement to trace their activities. These transactions are common in ransomware attacks, dark web marketplaces, and illicit online trade.

Example: Bitcoin in Ransomware Payments (2020)

In 2020, a ransomware attack targeted **Indian hospitals**, demanding ransom payments in **Bitcoin**. The attackers encrypted hospital records and systems, knowing that Bitcoin would make it harder to trace the payments.

Bitcoin and Privacy Coins in Criminal Networks

Although **Bitcoin** is still widely used in criminal transactions, privacy-focused cryptocurrencies like **Monero** are gaining popularity because they provide enhanced anonymity. Unlike Bitcoin, which has a public ledger, Monero obscures both the sender and recipient, making it nearly impossible to trace.

Example: Monero Used in Dark Web Transactions (2021)

A 2021 report highlighted that **Monero** was becoming increasingly popular in dark web transactions due to its enhanced privacy features, making it difficult for law enforcement to track.

Key takeaways from this Chapter

As cyber criminals continue to innovate, they exploit new technologies and tactics to commit crimes on a global scale. The use of **malware, ransomware, spyware, social engineering attacks**, and the **dark web** has created an environment where individuals, businesses, and governments face constant cyber threats. Coupled with the rise of **cryptocurrency**, cyber criminals now have more tools than ever to operate anonymously and evade law enforcement. Understanding these methods and techniques is the first step in defending against cyber crime and developing robust security measures to protect critical data and systems.

References used in this Chapter

1. BBC. "WannaCry ransomware: What is it and how does it spread?" (https://www.bbc.com/news/technology-39901382)

2. Indian Express. "Petya ransomware: What is it and how does it work?" (https://indianexpress.com/article/technology/tech-news-technology/petya-ransomware-india-cyber-attacks-hacking-4727189/)

3. The Guardian. "WhatsApp sues Israeli firm over hacking claims" (https://www.theguardian.com/technology/2019/oct/30/whatsapp-pegasus-spyware-

indian-journalists-activists)

4. Times of India. "Phishing attacks on banks are on the rise" (https://timesofindia.indiatimes.com/business/ india-business/phishing-attacks-on-banks-are-on-the-rise/articleshow/66685012.cms)

5. The Hindu. "Aadhaar vishing scams: Fraudulent calls on the rise" (https://www.thehindu.com/news/national/ aadhaar-vishing-scams-fraudulent-calls-on-the-rise/ article30915477.ece)

6. Indian Express. "Mumbai University warns students about phishing emails" (https://indianexpress.com/ article/education/mumbai-university-phishing-email-attack-software-6054657/)

7. CNN. "AlphaBay, the largest dark web marketplace, shut down" (https://edition.cnn.com/2017/07/20/us/ alphabay-dark-web-shutdown/index.html)

8. Economic Times. "Over 1.3 million credit/debit card details of Indians up for sale on dark web" (https://economictimes.indiatimes.com/wealth/ borrow/over-1-3-million-credit-debit-card-details-of-indians-up-for-sale-on-dark-web/articleshow/ 71944690.cms)

9. Hindustan Times. "Hackers demand bitcoins as ransom from hospitals" (https://www.hindustantimes.com/ india-news/hackers-demand-bitcoins-as-ransom-from-hospitals/story-pbPkl7D0MmFgWaIswcLMHM.html)

10. Forbes. "Bitcoin vs Monero: Why criminals select Monero over other cryptocurrencies" (https://www.forbes.com/sites/stevenehrlich/2021/ 05/14/bitcoin-vs-monero-why-criminals-select-monero-over-other-cryptocurrencies/?sh=7d6203a4552b)

Legal Framework for Cyber Crime in India

Chapter 4: Legal Framework for Cyber Crime in India

With the rise of cyber crimes in India, a robust legal framework has been developed to combat the growing threat. India's legal system has established several laws and initiatives to regulate, prevent, and prosecute cyber crimes. These laws are aimed at safeguarding individuals, businesses, and national interests from cyber criminals. This chapter will provide a detailed overview of key cyber laws in India, including the IT Act, Data Protection laws, and international cooperation efforts, as well as the role of CERT-In (Indian Computer Emergency Response Team). In addition, we will explore the provisions of the Bharatiya Nyaya Sanhita, a new framework for addressing various aspects of criminal law in India.

IT Act, 2000: Key Provisions and Amendments

The Information Technology (IT) Act, 2000, was the first major step by the Indian government to address cyber crime and regulate electronic commerce. This Act is the cornerstone of India's cyber law framework, providing legal recognition to electronic transactions and combating various forms of cyber crimes.

Key Provisions of the IT Act, 2000

1. **Digital Signatures and Electronic Records**
    The IT Act gives legal recognition to digital signatures and electronic records, enabling businesses to transact

digitally with legally valid documents.

2. **Cyber Crimes and Punishments**
    Several sections of the IT Act deal with specific cyber crimes and their punishments:

    ◦ **Section 43**: Addresses unauthorized access to computer systems, data theft, and introducing viruses into computer networks. Offenders are liable for compensation.
    ◦ **Section 66**: Prescribes punishment for hacking and includes provisions for penalties for damage to computers, networks, and data.
    ◦ **Section 67**: Covers obscenity and pornography on digital platforms, prescribing punishment for publishing or transmitting obscene content online.

3. **Corporate Responsibility**
    The IT Act places liability on companies for security breaches under **Section 85**, which holds that companies may be held responsible for cyber crimes committed by employees if they fail to implement adequate security measures.

Amendments to the IT Act, 2008
The IT Act was amended in 2008 to address new and emerging cyber threats, such as data breaches, identity theft, and phishing. The key changes introduced by the 2008 amendments include:

• **Section 66A**: Introduced to criminalize sending offensive messages via communication services, but it was struck down by the Supreme Court in 2015 due to its vague wording and potential for misuse.

- **Section 66B**: Addresses punishment for dishonestly receiving stolen computers, mobile phones, or other electronic devices.
- **Section 66C**: Criminalizes identity theft and the fraudulent use of others' personal information.

The 2008 amendments also included provisions for cyber terrorism (Section 66F), providing for life imprisonment for those found guilty of hacking into sensitive government systems and threatening national security through cyber attacks.

Data Protection and Privacy Laws

In an era where data breaches are common and personal information is increasingly stored online, data protection and privacy laws have become vital. India has recognized the need for strong data protection laws to safeguard personal and sensitive data from unauthorized access and misuse.

Personal Data Protection Bill, 2019

The **Personal Data Protection Bill, 2019** (PDP Bill) was introduced in the Indian Parliament to establish a comprehensive framework for data protection. The bill proposes to regulate the collection, storage, and use of personal data and sets guidelines for ensuring user privacy.

Key Provisions of the Personal Data Protection Bill

- **Definition of Personal Data**: The bill defines personal data as any information that can identify an individual, either directly or indirectly.
- **Data Localization**: The bill mandates that sensitive personal data must be stored within India. This provision aims to ensure that Indian citizens' data is protected and subject to Indian laws.

- **Data Fiduciaries**: The bill introduces the concept of data fiduciaries, entities that collect and process personal data. These fiduciaries must adhere to stringent data protection standards and are responsible for protecting users' data.
- **Consent**: Explicit consent from individuals is required before processing their personal data. Data fiduciaries are required to inform users of the purpose for which their data is being collected and used.
- **Penalties**: The bill proposes significant penalties for non-compliance. Organizations that fail to protect users' data or violate the bill's provisions may face fines of up to ₹15 crore or 4% of their global turnover.

The Personal Data Protection Bill is still under discussion and may undergo revisions, but it represents a major step toward ensuring data privacy and security in India.

International Cyber Laws and Cooperation

Cyber crimes often transcend national boundaries, making international cooperation essential to combat global cyber threats. India actively participates in global initiatives and has bilateral agreements with various countries to strengthen its cyber security framework.

UN Initiatives and Bilateral Agreements

India is involved in several international forums aimed at strengthening cyber security and combating cyber crime. These include:

- **UN General Assembly's Resolution on Cybersecurity**: India has been a key participant in UN efforts to establish norms and principles for responsible behavior in cyberspace. The resolution encourages member states to adopt measures to prevent cyber attacks on critical infrastructure.

- **Bilateral Agreements**: India has signed several bilateral agreements with countries such as the United States, Japan, and Israel to collaborate on cyber security initiatives. These agreements cover areas like information sharing, joint investigations, and capacity building to combat cross-border cyber crimes.
- **Budapest Convention**: While India is not a signatory to the Budapest Convention on Cybercrime, the country engages with its principles. The convention provides a framework for international cooperation in investigating and prosecuting cyber crimes.

Role of CERT-In (Indian Computer Emergency Response Team)

The **Indian Computer Emergency Response Team (CERT-In)** is the national agency responsible for coordinating responses to cyber security incidents. Established in 2004 under the Ministry of Electronics and Information Technology, CERT-In plays a critical role in preventing, detecting, and responding to cyber threats across the country.

Structure and Functions of CERT-In

CERT-In's primary functions include:

- **Monitoring Cyber Security Incidents**: CERT-In continuously monitors cyber threats and vulnerabilities across the country. The agency analyzes cyber security incidents and issues advisories to government bodies and private organizations on how to protect their systems.

- **Incident Response**: CERT-In provides assistance to individuals and organizations in responding to cyber incidents. This includes analyzing the nature of attacks, helping recover compromised systems, and providing recommendations for securing networks.
- **Coordination with Law Enforcement**: CERT-In collaborates with law enforcement agencies and other government departments to investigate cyber crimes. It also liaises with international cyber security organizations to track global cyber threats.
- **Capacity Building**: CERT-In conducts training programs and workshops for government officials, corporate entities, and individuals to raise awareness about cyber security. These programs help strengthen India's cyber security infrastructure by building a skilled workforce capable of preventing and mitigating cyber threats.
- **Cyber Security Advisories**: CERT-In regularly publishes advisories on vulnerabilities, attacks, and best practices for securing IT systems. These advisories are used by businesses, government agencies, and individuals to protect their data and networks from cyber threats.

The Bharatiya Nyaya Sanhita (Indian Penal Code Reforms)

The Bharatiya Nyaya Sanhita (BNS), 2023, represents a significant overhaul of India's criminal justice system, replacing the Indian Penal Code (IPC) with a modernized legal framework. This new code aims to address contemporary challenges, including the rise of cyber crimes. As digital technology becomes increasingly integral to daily life, the need for robust legal mechanisms to combat cyber crimes has never been more critical. This write-up explores the provisions of the BNS related to cyber crimes, their implications, and how they complement existing laws like the Information Technology (IT) Act, 2000.

Key Provisions of BNS Addressing Cyber Crimes

1. **Section 294: Publication and Transmission of Obscene Material**

Section 294 of the BNS addresses the publication and transmission of obscene material, including electronic forms. This provision is crucial in combating the spread of explicit content online, which can have severe social and psychological impacts. The punishment includes imprisonment and fines, with harsher penalties for repeat offenders. This section aims to deter individuals from engaging in the distribution of obscene material, thereby protecting societal morals and individual dignity.

1. **Section 77: Voyeurism**

Section 77 specifically deals with capturing or publishing pictures of private parts or acts of a woman without her consent, constituting "voyeurism." This provision is vital in protecting individuals' privacy and dignity in the digital age, where unauthorized sharing of intimate images can lead to severe emotional distress and reputational damage. The section imposes stringent penalties to deter such invasive acts.

3. **Section 303: Cyber Theft**

Section 303 addresses theft related to mobile phones, data, or computer hardware/software. It provides a legal framework to prosecute individuals engaged in cyber theft activities. This section is particularly relevant in an era where data is a valuable asset, and its theft can lead to significant financial and personal losses. However, the applicability of special laws like the IT Act takes precedence in cases where they are attracted, ensuring a comprehensive legal approach to cyber theft.

4. Section 78: Cyber Stalking

Section 78 addresses the offense of stalking in both physical and cyber forms. It imposes imprisonment and fines for monitoring or bothering a woman through physical or electronic means. This provision is crucial in protecting individuals from harassment and ensuring their safety in both physical and digital spaces.

5. Section 317: Possession of Stolen Property

Section 317 applies when an individual receives stolen mobile phones, computers, or data. It imposes punishment for even the possession of such property, including by third parties. This section aims to curb the market for stolen digital goods and deter individuals from engaging in or facilitating cyber theft.

6. Section 318: Cyber Fraud

Section 318 addresses various forms of cyber fraud, including password theft, creation of bogus websites, and other deceptive practices conducted through digital means.

It imposes varying imprisonment and fines based on the gravity of the offense. This provision is essential in protecting individuals and organizations from financial losses and maintaining trust in digital transactions.

7. Section 336: Email Spoofing and Online Forgery

Section 336 deals with offenses like email spoofing and online forgery. It imposes imprisonment, fines, or both for individuals engaging in these deceptive practices. This section also applies when forgery aims to harm a person's reputation, ensuring comprehensive protection against digital deception.

8. Section 356: Defamation

Section 356 penalizes defamation, including sending defamatory content through email. It imposes imprisonment and fines, protecting individuals from reputational harm caused by false and malicious digital communications.

Punishment for Cyber Crimes under the IT Act

While the BNS provides a robust framework for addressing cyber crimes, the IT Act, 2000, remains the primary legislation governing cyber activities in India. The IT Act includes several provisions specifically targeting cyber crimes:

1. Section 72 and 72A: Breach of Confidentiality and Privacy

Sections 72 and 72A of the IT Act address unlawful acts related to the disclosure of information in violation of lawful contracts and breaches of confidentiality and privacy. These sections impose penalties for unauthorized acquisition and use of confidential information, protecting individuals' privacy and data security.

2. Section 43: Data Theft

Section 43 encompasses a range of activities falling under data theft. It specifies that individuals who, without proper authorization, download, copy, or extract data, computer databases, or information from a computer system or network, including data stored in removable storage media, are liable to compensate the affected party for damages. This provision is crucial in protecting digital assets and ensuring accountability for unauthorized data access.

Challenges and Ambiguities

While the BNS and the IT Act provide comprehensive legal frameworks for addressing cyber crimes, several challenges and ambiguities remain:

1. Definition Clarity

The lack of a clear definition for "cyber crimes" in the BNS can lead to interpretational issues. A precise definition is essential to ensure consistent application of the law and avoid ambiguities in legal proceedings.

2. Overlap with IT Act

The BNS complements the IT Act but may lead to overlapping jurisdictions and legal complexities. Harmonizing the provisions of the BNS with the IT Act is crucial to ensure a seamless legal approach to cyber crimes.

3. Enforcement Challenges

Effective enforcement of cyber crime laws requires specialized knowledge and resources. Law enforcement agencies must be adequately trained and equipped to handle the complexities of cyber investigations and prosecutions.

4. International Cooperation

Cyber crimes often transcend national borders, necessitating international cooperation for effective enforcement. Strengthening international legal frameworks and collaboration is essential to combat cross-border cyber crimes.

CHAPTER V

Investigating Cyber Crimes in India

The investigation of cyber crimes in India requires a specialized approach involving digital forensics, law enforcement coordination, and navigating legal complexities. The methods, tools, and challenges associated with these investigations are unique and require both technical expertise and international cooperation. This chapter will provide an in-depth look into the various aspects of cyber crime investigations, focusing on the collection of digital evidence, the role of different law enforcement agencies, and the challenges that arise in these cases.

Forensics in Cyber Crime Investigations

Forensic investigations are the backbone of solving cyber crimes. Cyber forensics involves collecting, preserving, and analyzing digital evidence in a legally sound manner. Given that most cyber crimes are conducted digitally, collecting reliable and admissible evidence is critical to solving cases and bringing perpetrators to justice.

Digital Evidence Collection

Digital evidence plays a crucial role in any cyber crime investigation. However, collecting digital evidence requires a systematic approach that ensures the integrity of the data is maintained. Digital evidence can come in various forms, including emails, files, metadata, browsing history, logs, and more. Investigators use a combination of hardware and software tools to extract and analyze this evidence.

Types of Digital Evidence

1. **Network Traffic**: Investigators often analyze network traffic to track malicious activities such as unauthorized access, data theft, or malware deployment. Logs from routers, firewalls, and intrusion detection systems can provide crucial evidence of the attacker's methods and origin.

2. **Emails and Communications**: Emails are often used as evidence in cases involving phishing, fraud, and impersonation. Forensic experts trace the source of suspicious emails by analyzing the header information, including IP addresses and routing paths.

3. **File Metadata**: File metadata, such as creation and modification dates, can provide insights into the timeline of the crime. It can also reveal information about who created the file, which system it was created on, and when it was accessed or altered.

Process of Digital Evidence Collection

1. **Identification**: The first step in digital forensics is identifying the devices or systems involved in the crime. This could include desktops, mobile phones, network servers, or even cloud-based systems. Investigators assess the potential sources of evidence and develop a strategy for data extraction.

2. **Preservation**: Digital evidence is fragile and can be easily altered or deleted. To ensure the admissibility of evidence in court, investigators must preserve the original data without tampering. This is typically done by creating a forensic image (an exact copy) of the data, which is then used for analysis while keeping the original data intact.

3. **Acquisition and Extraction:** Once the data has been preserved, forensic investigators use specialized tools like EnCase, FTK (Forensic Toolkit), and open-source tools like Autopsy to extract the necessary data. This includes recovering deleted files, extracting system logs, and identifying hidden or encrypted files.

4. **Analysis:** After data is extracted, forensic investigators analyze the data to identify suspicious activities, trace the attacker's path, and gather supporting evidence. Analysis may involve examining file systems, searching for malware, and analyzing network activity.

5. **Documentation and Reporting:** The final step in digital forensics is documenting the findings. Investigators create detailed reports outlining the methods used, the evidence collected, and the conclusions drawn. These reports must be clear and well-documented to be admissible in court.

Challenges in Cyber Forensics

Despite the importance of digital forensics in solving cyber crimes, investigators face a variety of challenges that can hinder their ability to collect and analyze evidence effectively.

1. Data Encryption

Cyber criminals often use encryption to protect their data from being accessed by investigators. Encryption converts data into a code that can only be accessed or decrypted with a key, which is often kept secret by the criminal. Breaking encryption, especially strong encryption algorithms like AES (Advanced Encryption Standard), can take years without access to the decryption key, significantly delaying the investigation.

2. Data Volatility

Digital evidence is highly volatile, meaning it can be easily altered or destroyed. For instance, data stored in RAM (Random Access Memory) is lost when a system is powered off, making it difficult to preserve certain types of evidence. Cyber criminals can also use self-destructing malware or data-wiping software to erase incriminating evidence before investigators can collect it.

3. Cloud Computing

The rise of cloud computing adds another layer of complexity to digital forensics. Cloud data can be distributed across multiple servers located in different geographic regions, raising jurisdictional and legal issues. Moreover, investigators often require cooperation from cloud service providers, who may be subject to privacy laws in other countries, further complicating the evidence collection process.

4. Volume of Data

The sheer volume of data generated by digital devices can be overwhelming for forensic investigators. A single device can store terabytes of data, and investigators must sift through all of it to find relevant evidence. Tools like artificial intelligence (AI) and machine learning (ML) are increasingly being used to help automate the analysis of large datasets, but the process remains time-consuming.

Role of Law Enforcement

In India, several law enforcement agencies play pivotal roles in investigating cyber crimes. These agencies must coordinate at local, national, and international levels to handle cases that often cross jurisdictions and involve complex digital networks.

Key Agencies and Their Roles

1. **Cyber Crime Cells**: Cyber crime cells operate at the state and district levels and are the first point of contact for citizens reporting cyber crimes. These cells specialize in investigating cases such as online fraud, phishing, identity theft, and cyberstalking. Cyber crime cells work closely with local police and provide technical expertise in handling cyber-related cases.

2. **Central Bureau of Investigation (CBI)**: The CBI's **Cyber Crime Investigation Division** handles high-profile cyber crime cases that require national attention. The CBI often steps in for cases involving major financial fraud, data breaches, and crimes that involve cross-border elements. The agency works closely with other national agencies and foreign counterparts to conduct thorough investigations.

3. **National Investigation Agency (NIA)**: The NIA is responsible for investigating cases of cyber terrorism, where national security is at stake. The NIA investigates cyber attacks targeting critical infrastructure, government systems, and incidents where cyber warfare tactics are used. The NIA also monitors threats posed by foreign cyber espionage groups.

4. **Indian Computer Emergency Response Team (CERT-In)**: Although CERT-In is primarily responsible for monitoring and responding to cybersecurity incidents, it plays a critical role in cyber crime investigations. CERT-In assists law enforcement agencies by identifying vulnerabilities, issuing advisories, and providing technical assistance in mitigating cyber attacks.

Example: After the Mumbai power grid attack in 2020, CERT-In worked closely with state-level cyber cells, the

NIA, and the Ministry of Home Affairs to investigate the source of the attack, which was later traced to a foreign hacker group. CERT-In's expertise in cybersecurity allowed law enforcement agencies to respond quickly and prevent further damage to the country's critical infrastructure.

Coordination with International Law Enforcement

Since many cyber crimes involve perpetrators operating from foreign jurisdictions, international cooperation is vital in bringing these criminals to justice. Indian law enforcement agencies frequently collaborate with international agencies to exchange information, conduct joint investigations, and secure the extradition of criminals.

Mechanisms of International Cooperation:

1. **Interpol and Europol:** These international law enforcement agencies facilitate global cooperation on cyber crime investigations. Through Interpol and Europol, India can share information, request assistance, and collaborate on cross-border investigations. These agencies also maintain databases of known cyber criminals, allowing countries to identify and track suspects.

2. **Mutual Legal Assistance Treaties (MLATs):** India has signed MLATs with several countries to facilitate cooperation in legal matters, including cyber crime investigations. MLATs allow law enforcement agencies to request evidence, such as data stored on foreign servers, and collaborate with foreign governments to prosecute cyber criminals.

3. **Bilateral Agreements:** India has entered into bilateral cybersecurity agreements with countries like the United States, Japan, and Israel to promote collaboration on

cyber crime investigations. These agreements encourage information sharing, joint training programs, and coordination during investigations of transnational cyber crimes.

Example: In 2016, the Bangladesh Bank heist demonstrated the importance of international cooperation in cyber crime investigations. Hackers attempted to steal $81 million from the bank's account at the Federal Reserve Bank of New York using fraudulent SWIFT (Society for Worldwide Interbank Financial Telecommunications) transactions. The investigation required cooperation between law enforcement agencies in India, the U.S., and Bangladesh, as the hackers were operating from different countries.

Challenges in Investigation

While law enforcement agencies in India have made significant strides in combating cyber crime, they continue to face numerous challenges in the investigation process. These challenges stem from the rapid evolution of technology, jurisdictional issues, and a lack of resources.

Lack of Technical Expertise

One of the most significant challenges facing Indian law enforcement agencies is the lack of technical expertise in handling complex cyber crimes. Unlike traditional crimes, cyber crimes require a deep understanding of digital forensics, encryption, and network security.

1. Skill Gap

Many law enforcement personnel, especially at the local level, lack the necessary training to investigate cyber crimes effectively. This skill gap limits their ability to collect and analyze digital evidence, particularly in cases involving sophisticated attackers.

2. Limited Access to Advanced Tools

In addition to the skill gap, many cyber crime cells and police departments lack access to cutting-edge forensic tools. Without these tools, investigators cannot recover deleted files, analyze encrypted data, or trace digital footprints effectively.

Example: In the Aadhaar data breach case, the investigation faced delays due to the technical complexity of the breach and the lack of specialized expertise in handling large-scale data leaks. While forensic investigators eventually uncovered the methods used by the attackers, the investigation would have progressed faster with better training and access to modern forensic tools.

Cross-border Crimes and Jurisdictional Issues

Cyber crimes often span multiple countries, making it difficult for a single country's law enforcement agencies to investigate and prosecute the criminals. These cross-border crimes present unique challenges in terms of legal jurisdiction and cooperation between nations.

1. Jurisdictional Conflicts

Each country has its own legal framework for cyber crimes, and investigating cross-border crimes requires navigating multiple legal systems. Cyber criminals often take advantage of these jurisdictional issues by operating from countries with weak cyber crime laws or those that do not cooperate with international law enforcement.

2. Data Localization

Another challenge arises from the fact that digital evidence, such as data stored in the cloud, may be hosted on servers located in multiple countries. Accessing this data requires cooperation from foreign governments and service providers, which can be a lengthy process. Data localization laws, which require data to be stored within a country's borders, also create hurdles in cross-border investigations.

Example: In the 2016 Bangladesh Bank heist, the cyber criminals were able to steal $81 million by exploiting international banking systems. Since the attackers operated from multiple countries and used servers based in different jurisdictions, law enforcement agencies from several nations had to coordinate to track the funds and bring the criminals to justice. This case highlighted the complexity of investigating cyber crimes that involve multiple jurisdictions.

Key takeaways from this Chapter

Investigating cyber crimes in India is a multifaceted process that requires advanced forensic tools, collaboration between multiple law enforcement agencies, and international cooperation. Cyber crime cells, the CBI, NIA, and CERT-In play vital roles in investigating and responding to cyber crimes. However, they face significant challenges, such as a lack of technical expertise and the complexities of cross-border jurisdictional issues. To address these challenges, Indian law enforcement agencies must invest in capacity building, modern forensic tools, and strengthening cooperation with international counterparts. By addressing these challenges, India can improve its ability to investigate and combat the ever-evolving threat of cyber crime.

CHAPTER VI

Cyber Security Strategies and Solutions

Cybersecurity has become one of the most critical areas of focus for individuals, businesses, and governments alike as digital technology penetrates every aspect of modern life. Cyber attacks can lead to massive financial losses, reputational damage, and national security threats. This chapter provides an in-depth examination of strategies and solutions aimed at combating cyber crime, focusing on best practices for individuals and businesses, securing critical infrastructure, and leveraging advanced technologies such as artificial intelligence (AI) and big data analytics in cyber crime prevention.

Best Practices for Individuals and Businesses

The cornerstone of cybersecurity begins with individuals and businesses adopting best practices to safeguard their data, devices, and systems from cyber threats. These practices form the foundation for a resilient digital environment and mitigate many common cyber attacks.

Password Hygiene and Multi-factor Authentication (MFA)

Password Hygiene

Weak passwords are one of the most common entry points for cyber criminals, especially in brute force attacks, where automated systems are used to guess passwords, and credential-stuffing attacks, where hackers use previously leaked credentials to access accounts. This makes strong password hygiene a critical defense.

Advanced Best Practices for Password Hygiene:

1. **Use Long Passphrases**: A passphrase (a combination of random words or phrases) is generally more secure than a simple password. For example, "SunriseJupiterSky22!" is both easy to remember and difficult for hackers to crack.

2. **Enable Passwordless Authentication**: Some systems now offer passwordless authentication using biometric verification (fingerprints or facial recognition) or security keys, which remove the risk of password theft altogether. Passwordless authentication is emerging as a highly secure alternative to traditional passwords.

3. **Regularly Change Passwords**: While password changes have become less emphasized in recent years (due to password fatigue), regularly updating critical passwords—such as those for banking, email, and work accounts—can prevent ongoing threats in case of unnoticed breaches.

Multi-factor Authentication (MFA)

Multi-factor authentication (MFA) has become the gold standard for securing sensitive accounts. MFA requires users to provide two or more types of verification, typically combining a password with something the user has (such as a smartphone) or something the user is (such as a fingerprint).

More Advanced MFA Solutions:

- **FIDO2 and WebAuthn**: These are emerging standards for passwordless login methods that involve public-key cryptography and hardware tokens such as YubiKeys.

They are designed to protect against phishing and other types of attacks where credentials can be intercepted.

- **Adaptive MFA**: This method dynamically adjusts the level of authentication required based on the user's behavior, location, and other contextual factors. For instance, if a user logs in from a known location, they might only be asked for their password, but logging in from an unusual location might trigger the need for additional verification steps.

Example: The Colonial Pipeline ransomware attack (2021) highlighted the importance of MFA. Hackers accessed the company's system through a compromised password, leading to fuel shortages across the eastern United States. Had MFA been in place, the attackers would not have been able to breach the network with just a password.

Secure Browsing and Communication Tools

The internet is rife with vulnerabilities that cyber criminals exploit to steal data, spread malware, and compromise networks. By adopting secure browsing habits and utilizing secure communication tools, both individuals and businesses can significantly reduce their exposure to cyber threats.

Advanced Secure Browsing Practices

1. **DNS-over-HTTPS (DoH)**: DoH encrypts DNS requests (the process that translates domain names into IP addresses), preventing attackers from intercepting and manipulating DNS queries. This reduces the risk of DNS spoofing, where a hacker redirects users to malicious websites.

2. **Browser Isolation**: This technique isolates the user's browsing activity from the rest of the system, ensuring that any malicious code executed during browsing remains quarantined and cannot affect the broader network.

3. **Zero Trust Browsing**: This approach treats every website and connection as potentially hostile. It involves strict access controls, blocking potentially risky websites, and restricting the actions users can perform while browsing, such as downloading files or filling out forms on unverified websites.

Advanced Secure Communication Tools

1. **Quantum-safe Encryption**: As quantum computing advances, current encryption methods may become vulnerable. Some secure communication tools are beginning to implement quantum-safe encryption protocols to future-proof against quantum-powered attacks.

2. **Secure Collaboration Platforms**: Tools such as Signal, Wire, and Microsoft Teams offer end-to-end encryption for text, voice, and video communication. These platforms are increasingly favored in business settings for ensuring that sensitive communications remain private.

3. **Encrypted File Sharing**: Tools like Tresorit and Sync provide end-to-end encryption for sharing files over the cloud, ensuring that data is protected even during transmission. They also offer control over file access and usage, allowing users to revoke access when needed.

Example: In the case of Zoom bombing (2020), where uninvited participants disrupted Zoom meetings with inappropriate content, secure communication practices such as enabling password-protected meetings, restricting screen sharing, and using end-to-end encryption were later recommended to secure virtual gatherings.

Securing Critical Infrastructure

Critical infrastructure is essential for the functioning of a modern society, including energy, water, transportation, and financial services. These systems are increasingly becoming targets of cyber attacks, as disruptions can have widespread societal and economic consequences.

Government Initiatives for Cyber Security

The protection of critical infrastructure from cyber attacks has become a top priority for governments worldwide. Governments are implementing policies, launching cybersecurity frameworks, and setting up dedicated organizations to oversee the security of critical infrastructure.

Cyber Security Policy Updates

Many countries, including India, are constantly updating their national cybersecurity policies to reflect the changing nature of cyber threats. New initiatives focus on threat intelligence sharing, incident response, and increasing cyber awareness across all levels of government and industry.

- **India's National Cyber Security Strategy (NCSS):** An upcoming update to India's **National Cyber Security Policy** (which is expected to replace the 2013 policy) will emphasize securing critical infrastructure, expanding the cyber workforce, and promoting international cooperation on cybersecurity. The strategy will also enhance India's capacity to respond to threats through improved cybersecurity laws and regulations.

Sector-Specific Security Standards

Certain sectors—like finance, healthcare, and energy—are subject to stricter cybersecurity regulations to ensure that critical services are protected from cyber threats.

- **Energy Sector**: The **Indian Smart Grid Task Force (ISGTF)** works on securing energy infrastructure by deploying robust cyber-physical security standards across the smart grid. With more energy systems becoming automated, smart grid security is essential to prevent attacks on power supply systems.
- **Banking Sector**: The **Reserve Bank of India (RBI)** mandates that banks implement strong cybersecurity frameworks to protect against growing threats, especially related to digital payments and online banking.

Example: The NotPetya attack (2017), which targeted Ukraine's power grid, financial institutions, and government agencies, demonstrated the devastating impact that cyber attacks on critical infrastructure can have. The attack disrupted vital services and led to significant economic losses globally.

Public-Private Partnerships in Cyber Security

Public-private partnerships (PPPs) are key to strengthening the cybersecurity posture of nations. The private sector, particularly companies in technology, telecommunications, and finance, holds vast amounts of data and infrastructure that must be secured. Collaboration between the public and private sectors is crucial for implementing effective cybersecurity measures.

Key Benefits of Public-Private Partnerships

1. **Information Sharing**: Governments and private companies can exchange threat intelligence, including information on new vulnerabilities, malware signatures, and indicators of compromise (IOCs). This enhances the ability of both sectors to detect and respond to cyber threats quickly.

2. **Incident Response Coordination**: In the event of a major cyber attack, coordinated incident response between public and private entities ensures faster containment and recovery. Such partnerships can also provide businesses with access to government resources, such as cybersecurity frameworks and expert consultation.

3. **Innovation in Security Solutions**: By working together, governments and private companies can develop cutting-edge security technologies. For example, public-private research collaborations can focus on enhancing AI-driven cybersecurity tools, improving encryption technologies, and building cyber resilience frameworks.

Example: The U.S. National Cybersecurity and Communications Integration Center (NCCIC) partners with private sector companies to facilitate cybersecurity information sharing and coordinate incident response efforts. NCCIC works closely with critical infrastructure operators to secure national assets from cyber attacks.

Role of AI and Big Data in Cyber Crime Prevention

With the rise in the volume and complexity of cyber threats, manual processes alone are insufficient to detect and respond to attacks in real time. AI and big data analytics are transforming cybersecurity by enabling proactive threat detection and faster, more accurate responses to cyber attacks.

AI-driven Threat Detection

AI-powered tools are rapidly becoming indispensable for detecting and mitigating cyber threats. These tools use machine learning algorithms to analyze vast amounts of data, identify patterns, and detect anomalies that may indicate malicious activity.

Advanced AI Techniques in Cybersecurity

1. **Behavioral Analysis**: AI can establish normal behavior patterns for users, devices, and networks. Any deviations from these patterns—such as unusual login attempts or abnormal file access—can be flagged as potential threats. This allows for more proactive detection of threats, especially insider threats or compromised accounts.

2. **Threat Intelligence Platforms**: AI-driven threat intelligence platforms gather and analyze data from millions of sources, including open-source threat feeds, dark web forums, and social media. By correlating this information with known attack patterns, AI can predict emerging threats and provide actionable insights to cybersecurity teams.

3. **AI in Security Operations Centers (SOCs)**: Many SOCs are integrating AI-driven tools to automate threat detection, risk assessment, and incident response. AI can filter out false positives, prioritize genuine threats, and even suggest response actions for security analysts,

reducing the workload on human operators.

Example: AI tools were instrumental in identifying the SolarWinds supply chain attack in 2020. AI systems analyzing network traffic noticed unusual activity, which led to the discovery of the massive breach that had compromised multiple U.S. government agencies and private companies.

Big Data Analytics for Monitoring Suspicious Activities

Big data analytics offers organizations the ability to process and analyze massive volumes of data, allowing for comprehensive monitoring of network traffic and user behavior to identify potential cyber threats.

Big Data Use Cases in Cybersecurity

1. **Anomaly Detection**: By analyzing vast amounts of network traffic and system logs, big data tools can identify deviations from the norm that may indicate a cyber attack. For example, an unusual increase in outbound traffic from a company's network could signal a data breach.

2. **Predictive Analytics**: Big data analytics can be used to build predictive models that anticipate future cyber attacks based on historical data. These models can identify patterns that are commonly associated with certain types of attacks, allowing organizations to proactively defend against them.

3. **Threat Hunting**: Security teams use big data analytics for threat hunting, a proactive approach to searching for signs of compromise within a network. Threat hunters analyze network logs, endpoint data, and application logs to find evidence of hidden attacks or latent malware

that has not yet triggered an alert.

Example: Financial institutions use big data analytics to combat fraud. For instance, banks monitor millions of credit card transactions in real time, using big data tools to detect anomalies such as unusual purchasing patterns that could indicate card theft or fraudulent transactions.

Key takeaways from this Chapter

The threat landscape for cyber crime continues to evolve, and so too must the strategies and solutions used to combat these threats. For individuals and businesses, best practices like strong password hygiene, multi-factor authentication, secure browsing, and communication tools form the first line of defense. For governments and industries, securing critical infrastructure through initiatives, partnerships, and emerging technologies is paramount to national security. Finally, the integration of AI and big data analytics into cybersecurity practices represents a powerful shift toward predictive, proactive, and efficient cyber crime prevention. By implementing these strategies, we can build a more resilient and secure digital ecosystem.

CHAPTER VII

Emerging Trends in Cyber Crime

Cyber crime is continuously evolving with the advancement of technology. Emerging trends in cyber crime reflect a world where criminals leverage cutting-edge innovations to commit crimes in increasingly sophisticated ways. As technology becomes more complex, so do the tools and techniques used by cyber criminals, leading to new forms of digital threats. This chapter explores the latest trends in cyber crime, including deepfakes, AI-driven crimes, cyber warfare, state-sponsored attacks, ransomware as a service (RaaS), and the growing use of cyber extortion and blackmail.

Deepfakes and AI-driven Cyber Crimes

Deepfakes represent one of the most significant emerging threats in the cyber world. Powered by artificial intelligence (AI), deepfakes are hyper-realistic synthetic media in which an individual's likeness is digitally altered or created from scratch. While initially developed for creative and entertainment purposes, deepfakes have quickly found their way into malicious use cases, ranging from political manipulation to personal fraud.

Using AI to Create Synthetic Identities

Artificial intelligence and machine learning technologies are now being used to create synthetic identities for the purpose of deception. These AI-generated identities can be difficult to detect as fake because they often combine real data (such as partial names or personal details from data breaches) with synthetic elements, including AI-generated profile pictures or credentials.

Deepfake Technology

Deepfake technology relies on neural networks, specifically **Generative Adversarial Networks (GANs)**, to manipulate images, videos, and voices. GANs consist of two neural networks: one generates fake content, and the other evaluates its authenticity. Through continuous iteration, the generator network creates more convincing fake content until the discriminator network can no longer distinguish it from real content.

Real-World Applications of Deepfakes in Cyber Crime

1. **Political Disinformation**: Deepfakes have been used in political campaigns to spread disinformation by creating fake videos of politicians making controversial statements. These deepfakes are designed to go viral on social media, influencing public opinion and undermining trust in political systems.

2. **Financial Fraud**: In one notable case, deepfake technology was used to impersonate a CEO's voice in a phone call to a senior executive, tricking the executive into transferring $243,000 to a fraudulent account. This demonstrates how deepfake audio, combined with social engineering tactics, can lead to financial losses for businesses.

3. **Identity Theft**: Deepfake profiles are now being used on social media platforms, dating apps, and job websites to create convincing personas for scams. Cyber criminals can create fake identities by stitching together AI-generated photos with publicly available information from social media profiles, making it harder for victims to detect fraud.

Case Study: The Role of Deepfakes in Election Meddling

During the 2020 U.S. elections, several deepfake videos circulated online, purporting to show candidates making inflammatory statements or engaging in questionable behavior. Although none of these videos gained widespread traction before they were debunked, the potential for deepfakes to influence future elections remains a growing concern. With the advent of social media, such videos can spread rapidly, and by the time they are proven fake, the damage may already be done.

Detection and Prevention of Deepfake Crimes

The rise of deepfakes has prompted the development of tools designed to detect and counteract these synthetic media manipulations.

AI-driven Detection Tools

1. **Forensic Analysis**: AI-based deepfake detection tools analyze subtle artifacts in video and audio that are often missed by the human eye or ear. For example, deepfakes can have inconsistencies in lighting, unnatural lip movements, or irregular blinking patterns.

2. **Blockchain for Verification**: Some developers are turning to blockchain technology to verify the authenticity of digital content. By creating a tamper-proof record of when and where videos or images were created, blockchain can help verify if a piece of media has been altered or is authentic.

Prevention Strategies

1. **Public Awareness Campaigns**: Governments and cybersecurity organizations have launched public

awareness campaigns to educate people about the dangers of deepfakes and how to identify them. The focus is on critical thinking and verifying the source of any suspicious content before sharing it.

2. **Legislation**: Several countries, including the U.S. and the European Union, have introduced or are considering legislation that criminalizes the malicious use of deepfake technology. Laws are also being proposed to hold social media platforms accountable for the rapid dissemination of fake media.

Cyber Warfare and Espionage

Cyber warfare refers to state-sponsored attacks on digital infrastructure, often aimed at disrupting national security, sabotaging critical infrastructure, or stealing sensitive information. As geopolitical tensions escalate, cyber warfare has emerged as a tool for countries to gain strategic advantages without engaging in conventional military conflict.

State-Sponsored Attacks

State-sponsored cyber attacks are often sophisticated, well-funded, and carried out by specialized hacker groups, sometimes referred to as Advanced Persistent Threats (APTs). These groups often work under the direction or with the support of national governments to target other countries' government systems, financial institutions, or critical infrastructure.

Common Objectives of State-Sponsored Cyber Attacks

1. **Espionage**: State-sponsored hackers engage in cyber espionage to steal classified government information, intellectual property, and trade secrets from rival

nations. For example, the Chinese APT group known as **APT41** has been implicated in numerous cyber espionage operations targeting sectors such as healthcare, telecommunications, and finance.

2. **Disruption of Critical Infrastructure**: State-sponsored attackers target infrastructure systems like power grids, transportation networks, and financial services to cause economic or societal chaos. A well-known example is the **Stuxnet virus** developed by the U.S. and Israel, which disrupted Iran's nuclear program by targeting its centrifuges.

3. **Election Interference**: Cyber attacks are increasingly being used as tools of election meddling. In 2016, Russian hackers infiltrated the U.S. Democratic National Committee (DNC) and leaked sensitive information in an attempt to sway the presidential election.

Cyber Warfare Case Study: The NotPetya Attack

The **NotPetya attack (2017)** is often cited as one of the most devastating state-sponsored cyber attacks. Believed to have originated in Russia, the malware was initially directed at Ukrainian businesses and government entities but quickly spread globally, affecting companies such as Maersk and Merck. The attack caused over $10 billion in damages and disrupted business operations worldwide. NotPetya encrypted files and demanded a ransom, though paying the ransom did not lead to data recovery.

International Cooperation in Combating Cyber Warfare

The global nature of cyber warfare necessitates international cooperation between governments and institutions. Several frameworks and treaties have been developed to manage the risks associated with cyber warfare and to create norms for responsible behavior in cyberspace.

NATO's Role in Cyber Defense

NATO has recognized cyber warfare as a key area of focus in its defense strategy. It has established a **Cyber Defense Pledge** that encourages member nations to strengthen their national cybersecurity capabilities and share intelligence related to cyber threats. NATO also operates a **Cyber Defense Center of Excellence** in Estonia, which focuses on research and the development of strategies to counteract cyber warfare.

United Nations' Cybersecurity Efforts

The **United Nations (UN)** has taken steps to regulate cyber activities through the **UN Group of Governmental Experts (UN GGE)**. The group has proposed norms and recommendations that promote state responsibility in cyberspace and discourage the use of offensive cyber capabilities. Although these recommendations are not legally binding, they represent a significant effort to establish global standards in cybersecurity.

Ransomware as a Service (RaaS)

Ransomware as a Service (RaaS) has transformed ransomware attacks into a full-fledged business model, allowing even non-technical criminals to launch ransomware attacks. RaaS platforms provide ready-made ransomware kits that can be leased by cyber criminals in exchange for a portion of the profits.

How RaaS Works

RaaS follows the Software as a Service (SaaS) business model, where developers create ransomware programs and sell or lease them to other cyber criminals, typically through dark web forums. These operators do not need to develop the ransomware themselves; instead, they pay a fee to use an already-developed toolkit and then launch their attacks on selected targets.

Components of a RaaS Platform

1. **Ransomware Kit**: The core of the RaaS model is the ransomware kit itself, which includes malware capable of encrypting a victim's files and demanding ransom. Many kits come with customizable features, such as the ability to set the ransom amount and determine which types of files to target.
2. **Affiliate Program**: RaaS platforms operate on an affiliate model, where operators (criminals) lease the software from developers in exchange for a percentage of the ransom payments. For example, an operator may earn 70% of the ransom, while the developer retains the remaining 30%.
3. **Payment Portal**: RaaS platforms provide secure payment portals, often utilizing cryptocurrencies like Bitcoin, to ensure anonymity and facilitate ransom payments. These platforms may even provide customer service to ensure smooth transactions between victims and attackers.

RaaS in Action: The DarkSide Ransomware Attack

The **DarkSide ransomware group** made headlines in 2021 after launching a successful attack on **Colonial Pipeline**, the largest fuel pipeline in the United States. DarkSide operates as an RaaS platform, and it is believed that one of its affiliates carried out the attack. The ransomware shut down the pipeline for several days, leading to fuel shortages across the eastern U.S. and prompting the company to pay a ransom of $4.4 million.

Organized Crime in the Cyber World

The emergence of RaaS has highlighted the growing involvement of organized crime syndicates in the cyber world. Cyber crime has become highly professionalized, with different actors specializing in various aspects of an attack, such as developing malware, handling payment processing, or even offering technical support to victims.

Cyber Crime Syndicates

Many cyber crime syndicates now operate much like traditional businesses, with hierarchies, departments, and even service level agreements (SLAs). Some of these groups are based in regions with lax cybersecurity laws, allowing them to operate with relative impunity.

The Role of Dark Web Marketplaces

Dark web marketplaces play a central role in enabling organized cyber crime. These platforms offer a range of illicit services, from hacking tools and stolen data to RaaS and other forms of malware. In 2021, law enforcement agencies shut down **DarkMarket**, one of the largest underground markets for illegal goods and services, including ransomware kits and stolen credentials.

Example: The REvil ransomware group is another notorious RaaS operator that has targeted businesses, government agencies, and healthcare organizations worldwide. In 2021, REvil launched a high-profile attack on meat processing company JBS, demanding a ransom of $11 million. REvil is known for working with affiliates who carry out attacks using its ransomware toolkit in exchange for a cut of the profits.

Cyber Extortion and Blackmailing Trends

Cyber extortion involves cyber criminals threatening individuals or organizations with harm unless they pay a ransom or meet certain demands. While ransomware is one form of cyber extortion, other types include blackmailing, denial-of-service (DoS) extortion, and sextortion.

Blackmailing Through Data Breaches

Cyber criminals often threaten to publicly release sensitive or damaging data obtained through data breaches unless a ransom is paid. Blackmail schemes have become more common as companies store increasing amounts of sensitive data online, making them vulnerable to these types of attacks.

Data Breach Blackmail

1. **Double Extortion**: In a growing trend, ransomware attackers not only encrypt victims' data but also exfiltrate sensitive information. If the victim refuses to pay the ransom, the attackers threaten to publish the stolen data, a tactic known as double extortion.

2. **Corporate Blackmail**: Cyber criminals target large corporations, threatening to expose confidential business information, trade secrets, or sensitive client data if their demands are not met. The reputational and legal consequences of such leaks often compel companies to comply.

Example: In 2020, Cognizant Technology Solutions, a Fortune 500 company, fell victim to a Maze ransomware attack in which attackers encrypted its data and stole sensitive corporate information. The attackers threatened to publish the stolen data if the company did not pay the ransom, a clear case of double extortion.

Sextortion and Cyber Blackmailing

Sextortion involves cyber criminals blackmailing victims by threatening to release intimate photos, videos, or messages unless a ransom is paid. These crimes often target individuals, but they can also be used against businesses or high-profile public figures.

How Sextortion Works

Sextortion typically starts with hackers gaining access to a victim's private communications, either through social engineering, phishing, or malware. Once they have compromising materials, they threaten the victim with public exposure unless they comply with the attacker's demands, often asking for money or additional explicit content.

Prevention and Response

1. **Awareness Campaigns**: Several organizations, including law enforcement agencies, run awareness campaigns to educate individuals about the dangers of sextortion and the importance of safeguarding their digital privacy.

2. **Legislation and Law Enforcement**: Many countries have passed laws specifically targeting sextortion and cyber blackmail. Law enforcement agencies are working with international organizations to track and arrest individuals involved in these crimes, especially those operating across borders.

Example: In 2019, a sextortion campaign targeted thousands of victims worldwide. Cyber criminals sent emails claiming to have hacked their webcams and recorded intimate moments. The attackers threatened to release the footage unless victims paid a ransom in Bitcoin. In most cases, the hackers had not actually obtained any compromising footage, but the fear of exposure drove many victims to pay.

Key takeaways from this Chapter

Emerging trends in cyber crime reflect the ever-changing nature of the digital landscape. Cyber criminals are becoming more sophisticated, leveraging advanced technologies like AI to create deepfakes, organizing into well-funded cyber crime syndicates, and using ransomware as a service to carry out widespread attacks. Meanwhile, state-sponsored cyber warfare and espionage have become new battlegrounds for geopolitical conflicts, with significant implications for national security. As these threats evolve, so must the strategies and solutions to combat them. Governments, businesses, and individuals must remain vigilant, adopt advanced cybersecurity measures, and stay informed about emerging trends to protect themselves from the growing menace of cyber crime.

CHAPTER VIII

The Future of Cyber Crime in India

The digital landscape in India is rapidly expanding as the country embraces technological advancements and transitions to a digital economy. With this growth comes an increasing risk of cyber crime, as new technologies create opportunities for both innovation and exploitation. The future of cyber crime in India will be shaped by the evolving tactics of cyber criminals, advancements in cyber defense mechanisms, and the global effort to combat cyber threats. This chapter delves into the emerging techniques and threats in cyber crime, the importance of building a resilient cyber ecosystem, and India's evolving role in global cyber security efforts.

Evolving Techniques and New Threats

As technology advances, cyber criminals are constantly adapting their methods to exploit vulnerabilities in digital systems. New tools and techniques, many driven by cutting-edge technologies like quantum computing and artificial intelligence, are poised to transform the cyber crime landscape. This section examines the potential impact of these technologies and the new threats they pose to cyber security.

Quantum Computing and Its Impact on Cyber Security

Quantum computing is one of the most anticipated technological advancements of the 21st century, with the potential to revolutionize industries such as cryptography, medicine, and finance. However, this new era of computing also poses a significant threat to traditional cyber security measures, particularly encryption.

What is Quantum Computing?

Quantum computing is a type of computing that leverages the principles of quantum mechanics to perform calculations that are far more complex than those possible with classical computers. Unlike classical computers, which use bits to represent information as either 0 or 1, quantum computers use quantum bits, or **qubits**, which can exist in multiple states at once (a property known as **superposition**). This allows quantum computers to solve complex problems much faster than traditional computers.

The Threat to Encryption

Most modern encryption systems, such as **RSA** and **Elliptic Curve Cryptography (ECC)**, rely on the difficulty of factoring large prime numbers or solving discrete logarithmic problems, which are computationally hard for classical computers. Quantum computers, however, could break these encryption systems using algorithms like **Shor's algorithm**, which can efficiently factor large numbers.

- **RSA and Quantum Vulnerability**: RSA encryption, widely used for securing communications and transactions online, relies on the fact that it is computationally expensive for classical computers to factor large numbers. However, a sufficiently powerful quantum computer could break RSA encryption in a matter of seconds, rendering it obsolete.
- **ECC**: Similarly, Elliptic Curve Cryptography, used for securing many financial transactions and digital signatures, would also be vulnerable to quantum attacks, leading to widespread implications for the global financial system.

Quantum-resistant Encryption

To counter the potential threats posed by quantum computing, researchers are developing **post-quantum cryptography** (PQC) algorithms designed to withstand quantum attacks. These quantum-resistant encryption methods will be crucial in securing sensitive data once quantum computers become widely available.

- **Lattice-based Cryptography**: One promising approach is lattice-based cryptography, which relies on the hardness of lattice problems that are resistant to both classical and quantum algorithms. It is one of the leading candidates for post-quantum encryption.
- **Hash-based Signatures**: Another approach involves using hash-based digital signatures, which provide a quantum-resistant alternative to current signature schemes like RSA.

Potential Implications for India

India, like many other nations, relies heavily on digital infrastructure for sectors like finance, healthcare, and government services. Quantum computing poses a direct threat to this infrastructure if quantum-safe encryption is not implemented in time. India's move toward digital transformation through initiatives like **Digital India** means that quantum security will become a critical aspect of future cyber security planning.

Building a Resilient Cyber Ecosystem

A resilient cyber ecosystem is essential for India to defend against evolving cyber threats. This requires a multifaceted approach that includes strengthening legal frameworks, fostering public-private partnerships, improving cyber literacy, and investing in cyber security education and training.

Strengthening Legal Frameworks

India's current legal framework for cyber security is primarily based on the **Information Technology Act, 2000**, which has been amended over the years to address new challenges posed by cyber crime. However, as the nature of cyber threats evolves, so must the country's legal response.

The Need for Updated Cyber Laws

As cyber criminals adopt new methods, such as using AI for cyber attacks or launching ransomware attacks through **Ransomware as a Service (RaaS)** platforms, India's cyber laws must evolve to cover these emerging threats. Comprehensive legislation is needed to address areas such as:

- **Data Privacy**: With the rise of cloud computing and the increasing amount of personal data stored online, data privacy must be a core component of cyber legislation. The **Personal Data Protection Bill**, currently under consideration, aims to regulate how data is collected, stored, and shared, but more robust mechanisms will be needed to protect against evolving data breaches and privacy violations.
- **Cyber Crime and Punishment**: The legal system must impose stricter penalties for cyber criminals involved in large-scale attacks on critical infrastructure or financial systems. Additionally, laws must address newer forms of cyber crime, such as deepfakes, synthetic identity fraud, and quantum attacks.
- **Cross-border Cyber Crime**: As cyber crime increasingly crosses national borders, India must also enhance its international legal cooperation to address jurisdictional issues in prosecuting cyber criminals. This

includes signing **Mutual Legal Assistance Treaties (MLATs)** and collaborating with global cyber crime prevention initiatives.

Examples of Legal Initiatives

1. **Data Privacy Laws**: The **Personal Data Protection Bill, 2019** is a step toward establishing a comprehensive framework for protecting individuals' personal data. The bill introduces stricter regulations on data collection, storage, and usage, along with penalties for non-compliance.

2. **International Cooperation**: India has joined the **Budapest Convention on Cybercrime**, which seeks to promote cooperation between countries in prosecuting cyber criminals and developing shared legal standards. This will enhance India's ability to work with international partners to tackle cross-border cyber threats.

Encouraging Cyber Literacy and Education

As India becomes more digitally connected, it is essential to promote cyber literacy and ensure that individuals, businesses, and government entities understand how to protect themselves from cyber threats. Cyber security awareness campaigns, education programs, and training initiatives are necessary to build a more secure digital ecosystem.

The Importance of Cyber Literacy

Cyber literacy goes beyond basic digital literacy; it involves understanding the risks associated with online activities and knowing how to adopt best practices for personal and organizational security. This includes recognizing phishing attempts, maintaining secure passwords, updating software regularly, and understanding the importance of data privacy.

Cyber Education in Schools and Universities

To build a generation of cyber-aware citizens, India must integrate cyber security education into school curricula. Universities should also offer specialized programs in cyber security, AI ethics, and digital forensics to prepare students for careers in cyber defense.

- **Cyber Security Degree Programs**: Leading institutions like the **Indian Institute of Technology (IIT)** and the **National Institute of Technology (NIT)** are already offering specialized degrees and certification courses in cyber security. Expanding these programs and encouraging more students to enter the cyber security field will help address the growing demand for skilled professionals.

Government Initiatives for Cyber Literacy

The **National Cyber Security Policy, 2013** emphasizes the need for creating cyber security awareness among citizens and professionals. However, more needs to be done to ensure the effective implementation of these goals.

- **Cyber Swachhta Kendra**: This initiative, launched by **CERT-In**, aims to spread awareness about malware and botnet infections and offers tools to help individuals and businesses clean infected systems.
- **Cyber Surakshit Bharat Initiative**: This initiative focuses on creating awareness about cyber threats among government officials and aims to train them in best practices for securing government infrastructure.

Examples of Cyber Awareness Campaigns

1. **Cyber Jaagrukta Divas**: In 2020, the Ministry of Home Affairs launched the **Cyber Jaagrukta Divas (Cyber Awareness Day)** to educate citizens about cyber hygiene. On this day, various educational programs and awareness drives are conducted across the country, helping citizens understand how to protect themselves from online fraud, phishing, and ransomware.
2. **Public-Private Cyber Literacy Partnerships**: The government collaborates with private tech giants like **Google**, **Microsoft**, and **IBM** to host workshops and seminars on digital safety and cyber hygiene, targeting both rural and urban populations.

India's Role in Global Cyber Crime Prevention

As one of the fastest-growing digital economies, India is uniquely positioned to play a pivotal role in the global effort to combat cyber crime. India's contributions to international cyber security initiatives, coupled with its active participation in multilateral forums, demonstrate its commitment to addressing global cyber threats.

Contributions to International Cyber Security Initiatives

India's approach to cyber security has expanded from a domestic focus to becoming more integrated with global efforts. India has joined forces with several international organizations to bolster its cyber defenses and contribute to shaping global cyber security norms.

Collaborations with International Organizations

India collaborates with several international organizations and bodies that promote cyber security and combat global cyber crime. These collaborations help India stay ahead of emerging threats and foster cooperation with other nations.

1. **United Nations (UN)**: India actively participates in UN initiatives aimed at promoting peace and security in cyberspace. Through the **UN Group of Governmental Experts (UN GGE)** on developments in the field of information and telecommunications, India contributes to the formulation of guidelines that promote responsible state behavior in cyberspace.

2. **Bilateral and Multilateral Agreements**: India has signed bilateral cyber security agreements with countries such as the United States, Japan, and Israel. These agreements facilitate the sharing of threat intelligence, joint cyber defense exercises, and the development of cyber security frameworks.

India's Role in G20 Cyber Security Initiatives

India, as a member of the **G20**, has pushed for international cooperation on cyber crime prevention, particularly in areas related to financial crime and the protection of critical infrastructure. During G20 summits, India has emphasized the need for harmonized cyber laws, stronger data privacy regulations, and the creation of global frameworks for cyber threat intelligence sharing.

Case Study: India's Involvement in the Budapest Convention

While India is not a formal signatory to the **Budapest Convention**, the country has engaged with its principles and collaborates with signatory nations. The convention provides a framework for tackling cyber crime, including areas like child exploitation, computer-related fraud, and intellectual property violations.

The Road Ahead for India

As India continues to advance its digital infrastructure, the road ahead will require a strategic focus on building cyber resilience and developing stronger cyber security frameworks. The country's cyber ecosystem must evolve to address the increasing complexity and scale of cyber attacks. This involves improving both preventive measures and incident response capabilities.

Focus Areas for the Future

1. **Artificial Intelligence and Cyber Defense**: AI and machine learning will play an increasingly important role in detecting and mitigating cyber threats. India must invest in AI-powered cyber security solutions that can identify anomalies, detect breaches in real time, and respond automatically to cyber incidents.

2. **Post-Quantum Cryptography**: With the advent of quantum computing, India must prioritize the development and implementation of quantum-safe encryption methods. Early adoption of post-quantum cryptography will ensure that India remains protected from the potential quantum threats discussed earlier.

3. **Cyber Security Workforce Development**: India must continue to invest in building a skilled cyber security workforce. In addition to expanding university programs in cyber security, government and industry should collaborate to offer professional certification programs and on-the-job training in cutting-edge cyber defense techniques.

4. **Cyber Diplomacy**: Cyber diplomacy will become an essential tool in addressing global cyber crime. India must enhance its cyber diplomacy efforts by actively participating in international forums and negotiations

that aim to set norms and rules for responsible behavior in cyberspace.

Key takeaways from this Chapter

The future of cyber crime in India will be shaped by both the threats posed by emerging technologies and the steps taken by the government, industry, and civil society to build a resilient cyber ecosystem. As India continues to embrace digital transformation, it must remain vigilant in updating its legal frameworks, educating its population, and collaborating with global partners to tackle the ever-evolving landscape of cyber threats.

Common Cyber Frauds: Modus Operandi And Prevention

1. Fraud through Phishing Links

- **Modus Operandi:**

  - **Phishing** is one of the most common online frauds, where fraudsters trick individuals into revealing sensitive information (such as passwords, credit card details, or personal identification numbers) by pretending to be a legitimate entity like a bank, government agency, or well-known service provider.
  - Typically, the victim receives an email, text message, or social media message that appears to be from a trusted organization. The message often creates a sense of urgency (e.g., "Your account has been compromised" or "Please verify your identity to prevent service interruption").
  - The message contains a link that redirects the victim to a fake website that looks identical to the real website of the trusted organization. Once the victim enters their details (such as login credentials, banking information, etc.), the fraudster captures this information and uses it to gain access to the victim's accounts.
  - The fraudster may use the victim's information to steal money, make unauthorized purchases, or commit identity theft.

- **Prevention:**

  - Never click on links in unsolicited emails or

messages. Always type the website address directly into your browser.

○ Verify the URL of the website; phishing sites often have slight misspellings or additional characters.

○ Enable two-factor authentication (2FA) for your accounts whenever possible.

○ Use anti-phishing tools or browser extensions that can alert you to malicious sites.

2. Vishing Calls

• **Modus Operandi:**

○ **Vishing** (voice phishing) is a telephone-based scam where fraudsters impersonate legitimate entities, such as banks, government agencies, or companies, to trick victims into revealing sensitive personal and financial information.

○ Fraudsters often use social engineering tactics to create panic or urgency. For instance, they might tell the victim that there's been suspicious activity on their account, or that their bank account will be blocked unless they verify certain details immediately.

○ The fraudster will ask for personal information such as account numbers, credit card details, OTPs, passwords, or other sensitive data. Once they have this information, they can use it to carry out unauthorized transactions or steal the victim's identity.

○ In some advanced vishing scams, fraudsters use software that manipulates the caller ID (spoofing) to make it appear as though the call is coming from a legitimate source, like a bank or government agency.

- **Prevention**:

  - Never share personal or banking information over the phone, especially if you did not initiate the call.
  - Banks or legitimate agencies will never ask for your PIN, password, or OTP over the phone.
  - If you receive a suspicious call, hang up and contact the organization directly using a trusted phone number (not the number provided by the caller).
  - Register your number with your country's official "Do Not Disturb" or "Do Not Call" list to reduce spam calls.

3. Fraud using Online Marketplaces

- **Modus Operandi**:

  - Fraudsters exploit the growing popularity of online marketplaces by creating fake listings or posing as buyers or sellers on legitimate platforms.
  - In **seller scams**, fraudsters post items at significantly lower prices to attract buyers. The item may not exist, or it may be counterfeit. After the buyer makes the payment, the seller disappears without delivering the product.
  - In **buyer scams**, the fraudster pretends to be a buyer interested in an item the victim is selling. They may offer to pay via an online payment app or send a QR code for "payment." In reality, scanning the QR code debits money from the victim's account rather than crediting it.

- Fraudsters may also ask sellers to ship the product without payment, claiming that they will make the payment later or that a "third party" will handle it. Once the product is shipped, the fraudster vanishes.

- **Prevention:**

  - Use secure payment methods provided by the online marketplace platform. Avoid making payments outside the platform.
  - Be cautious of deals that seem too good to be true, especially items listed at significantly lower prices than market value.
  - Verify the reputation of the buyer or seller by reading reviews or checking their history on the platform.
  - Never share your bank account details, OTP, or scan QR codes for payment transactions when selling an item.

4. Credit Card Annual Fee Waiver - Fake Offer

- **Modus Operandi:**

  - In this scam, fraudsters call or send messages to credit card holders, claiming to represent the victim's credit card company. They offer to waive the annual fee or provide special discounts or offers.
  - The fraudster asks for the victim's credit card number, CVV, or OTP under the pretext of processing the waiver. They may claim that this information is needed for verification purposes or to initiate the offer.

- ○ Once the victim shares the details, the fraudster uses the card information to make unauthorized purchases or withdraw money.
- ○ Sometimes, the fraudster may even ask the victim to make a small payment (e.g., a processing fee), tricking them into paying money directly into the fraudster's account.

- **Prevention**:

  - ○ Never share your credit card details or OTP over the phone or through unsolicited messages.
  - ○ If you receive an offer for an annual fee waiver, contact your bank or credit card company directly to verify its legitimacy.
  - ○ Remember that banks will never ask for your CVV or OTP for such offers.
  - ○ Block suspicious numbers and report fraudulent calls to your bank or relevant authorities.

  ### 5. ATM Card Skimming Fraud

- **Modus Operandi**:

  - ○ **Skimming** occurs when fraudsters install small, hidden devices (skimmers) on ATM machines or POS terminals to steal the card details of unsuspecting users.
  - ○ The skimmer captures the magnetic stripe data of the card when it is inserted into the ATM or swiped at a POS terminal. Fraudsters often install a small camera or a fake keypad to capture the victim's PIN.
  - ○ Once the fraudster has the card details and PIN, they

create a cloned card and use it to withdraw money or make purchases without the victim's knowledge.

◦ Victims usually don't realize they've been scammed until they notice unauthorized transactions on their account.

- **Prevention**:

  ◦ Inspect the ATM or POS machine for any unusual attachments, loose parts, or signs of tampering before using it.

  ◦ Cover the keypad when entering your PIN to prevent anyone from seeing it.

  ◦ Use ATMs located in well-lit, high-traffic areas (preferably inside bank branches) to minimize the risk of tampered machines.

  ◦ Regularly monitor your bank account for unauthorized transactions and report suspicious activity immediately.

  ◦ Consider using ATMs that have chip-card readers rather than magnetic stripe readers, as they are more secure.

6. Fraud using Screen Sharing App/Remote Access

- **Modus Operandi**:

  ◦ In this type of fraud, fraudsters pose as customer service representatives or technical support agents from reputable organizations such as banks, e-commerce platforms, or telecom companies.

  ◦ The fraudster convinces the victim that there's an issue with their device (e.g., a security breach or a malfunction) that needs to be fixed remotely. They ask the victim to download and install a legitimate screen-sharing or remote access app like **TeamViewer, AnyDesk,** or **Zoho Assist**.

- Once the app is installed and the victim grants access, the fraudster can control the victim's device. This allows them to monitor the victim's banking activity, steal credentials, make unauthorized transactions, or even transfer money from the victim's account in real-time.
- In some cases, fraudsters make it appear as though they are "helping" the victim with a technical issue, while secretly stealing their data or transferring funds.

- **Prevention:**

  - Never install remote access apps on your device unless you trust the source completely and are 100% sure it is a legitimate request.
  - Legitimate organizations like banks or e-commerce companies will never ask for remote access to your device.
  - If you receive such a request, hang up and contact the organization directly through a verified customer service number.
  - If you have installed such an app unknowingly, immediately disconnect your device from the internet, uninstall the app, and inform your bank of any potential security breach.

7. SIM Swap/ SIM Cloning

- **Modus Operandi:**

  - In **SIM swap fraud**, fraudsters impersonate the victim and contact their mobile service provider, requesting a new SIM card. They claim the victim's original SIM has been lost or damaged. Fraudsters provide fake identification documents and complete the verification process with forged credentials.
  - Once the new SIM is activated, the fraudster gains control of the victim's phone number. This allows them to receive OTPs (One-Time Passwords) and security alerts sent by banks or other institutions, enabling unauthorized access to the victim's accounts.
  - The victim often realizes something is wrong when their phone loses network connectivity (as the original SIM becomes deactivated).
  - **SIM cloning** is another version of this fraud where the fraudster creates a duplicate SIM card using specialized software to intercept communications.

- **Prevention:**

  - Use two-factor authentication (2FA) for banking and other sensitive accounts, preferably through an authenticator app, rather than relying solely on SMS-based OTPs.
  - Register for alerts from your mobile service provider so that you are notified of any SIM card changes.
  - Contact your mobile service provider immediately if you experience an unexpected loss of service, as this could indicate that your SIM has been swapped.
  - Keep your personal information (like ID details and

phone numbers) private, and avoid sharing them with untrusted sources.

8. Frauds by Compromising Credentials through Search Engines

- **Modus Operandi:**

  - Fraudsters create fake customer service websites or advertisements that appear in search engine results when victims search for customer support contact numbers (such as for banks, airlines, or e-commerce platforms).
  - When the victim clicks on these fraudulent results, they are directed to a fake website or phone number where the fraudster pretends to be a legitimate representative.
  - The fraudster then convinces the victim to share sensitive information such as bank account numbers, card details, or OTPs, under the pretext of solving a problem or verifying their identity.
  - In some cases, fraudsters also install malware on the victim's device when they visit the fake website, which steals personal information.

- **Prevention:**

  - Always verify the authenticity of customer support contact numbers by visiting the official website of the organization directly, rather than relying on search engine results.
  - Be cautious of websites or ads that offer customer service numbers prominently, especially if they do

not match the official domain of the company.
- Install antivirus software and use browser extensions that block phishing websites to prevent accidentally visiting fraudulent sites.

9. Scam through QR Code Scan

- **Modus Operandi**:

  - Fraudsters exploit QR codes, which are commonly used for online payments and digital transactions. In this type of scam, fraudsters send a QR code to the victim, claiming it will be used to receive money (e.g., for a sale or a payment).
  - The victim, believing the QR code is for receiving funds, scans it with their payment app. However, the QR code is actually configured to **debit** money from the victim's account rather than crediting it.
  - The victim only realizes the scam after seeing that their bank account or digital wallet has been debited.

- **Prevention**:

  - Always verify the details of a transaction before scanning a QR code, especially when someone claims the code will be used to receive money. In reality, QR codes are primarily used to **pay** or **transfer** funds, not receive them.
  - Check transaction details carefully on your payment app before confirming any transaction.
  - Only deal with trusted individuals or businesses, and avoid scanning QR codes from unknown sources.

10. Impersonation through Social Media

- **Modus Operandi:**

  - Fraudsters hack or clone the social media accounts of the victim's friends or family members and send urgent messages asking for financial help (e.g., "I need money for an emergency" or "Please transfer money to this account").
  - The victim, believing the message is from a trusted friend or relative, transfers the money to the fraudster's account.
  - In some cases, the fraudster also asks for personal details such as bank account numbers or passwords under the pretext of needing help.
  - Once the money or personal information is shared, the fraudster vanishes, and the victim realizes that the real account holder was not involved.

- **Prevention:**

  - Be cautious of any urgent financial requests from friends or family over social media, especially if the request is out of character.
  - Verify the authenticity of the request by calling or messaging the person directly on another platform or phone number before sending any money or sharing personal information.
  - Enable two-factor authentication (2FA) on your social media accounts to prevent them from being hacked or cloned.
  - Be cautious about sharing sensitive personal information on social media platforms.

11. Juice Jacking – Stealing of Data through Charging Cable

- **Modus Operandi:**

  - **Juice jacking** occurs when fraudsters set up compromised public charging stations in locations such as airports, cafes, or shopping malls. These charging stations are connected to malicious hardware that is designed to steal data from the victim's device or install malware while it is charging.
  - When the victim plugs their phone or tablet into the charging station using a USB cable, the device's data (e.g., contacts, photos, passwords) may be accessed or copied without the victim's knowledge. In some cases, malicious software is installed on the device, allowing the fraudster to control or monitor the device remotely.
  - The victim is often unaware that their device has been compromised until they notice suspicious activity, such as unauthorized transactions or emails sent from their account.

- **Prevention:**

  - Avoid using public charging stations that rely on USB connections. If you need to charge your phone in a public place, use an electrical outlet and your own charging cable with an AC adapter.
  - Invest in a **USB data blocker** or **charge-only cable**, which prevents data transfer while allowing your device to charge.

- Regularly update your device's software to protect against malware and other security vulnerabilities.
- Keep sensitive personal and financial data stored securely, and avoid keeping it on your device if not necessary.

12. Lottery Fraud

- **Modus Operandi:**

  - Victims receive notifications via email, text message, or phone call claiming they have won a lottery, sweepstakes, or prize. The message typically comes with exciting news and uses branding that mimics legitimate organizations or lottery services.
  - To claim the "prize," victims are asked to pay processing fees, taxes, or administrative charges. In some cases, they may be asked to provide sensitive personal or financial information to verify their identity.
  - Once the victim makes the payment or provides their details, the fraudster either disappears, or they continue asking for more money under different pretexts (e.g., customs fees, legal fees).
  - The victim never receives the promised prize, and the money they sent is lost.

- **Prevention:**

  - Be cautious of unsolicited communications claiming you have won a lottery or prize, especially if you never entered the lottery.
  - Legitimate lotteries do not ask for fees or payments

to claim winnings. If payment is requested, it's likely a scam.
- Never share personal information (bank details, identification numbers) over email or phone to claim a prize.
- Verify the legitimacy of the lottery organization by checking its official website or contacting them directly.

13. Online Job Fraud

- **Modus Operandi:**

  - Fraudsters post fake job listings on online job portals, social media, or even email. These job offers often promise high salaries, attractive benefits, or flexible work-from-home opportunities.
  - Victims are typically asked to pay upfront fees for registration, training materials, or security deposits. Once the fee is paid, the fraudster vanishes, and the job offer turns out to be fake.
  - In some cases, fraudsters may collect personal information from job applicants (like bank account numbers, identification documents, or social security numbers) and use it for identity theft or fraudulent activities.
  - The victim either never hears back from the "employer" after making the payment or receives tasks that do not align with legitimate job responsibilities.

- **Prevention:**

- Be wary of job offers that sound too good to be true, especially those requiring payment for registration, training, or placement.
- Verify the legitimacy of the company by checking their official website and reading reviews from previous employees or applicants.
- Never share sensitive personal information during the initial stages of the application process.
- Legitimate employers do not require upfront payments or security deposits to offer a job.

14. Fake Account Number

- **Modus Operandi:**

  - In this type of fraud, fraudsters pose as legitimate businesses, service providers, or government agencies and provide the victim with a fake bank account number for making payments.
  - Victims, believing they are making a legitimate payment for goods or services, transfer money to the fraudster's bank account. The fraudster then disappears, and the victim never receives the product or service they paid for.
  - Fraudsters often create fake invoices, contracts, or communications to make the transaction appear legitimate.

- **Prevention:**

  - Always verify bank account details before making any large payments. Contact the business or service provider directly using official contact information to confirm the account number.

- Be cautious of unsolicited emails or messages requesting payment or providing a new account number for a transaction.
- If you receive a suspicious invoice or payment request, take extra steps to verify its legitimacy, especially if it involves large sums of money.

15. Fraud through Email (Phishing Emails)

- **Modus Operandi:**

  - Victims receive phishing emails that appear to come from trusted sources such as banks, government agencies, or well-known companies. These emails often ask the recipient to click on a link to resolve an issue with their account, reset a password, or verify their identity.
  - The link directs the victim to a fake website that mimics the appearance of a legitimate website. The victim is then asked to enter sensitive information such as login credentials, banking details, or passwords.
  - Once the fraudster obtains this information, they use it to access the victim's accounts, steal funds, or commit identity theft.
  - Some phishing emails also contain malicious attachments that, when opened, install malware on the victim's device, allowing the fraudster to steal personal data or monitor activity.

- **Prevention:**

- Avoid clicking on links or opening attachments in unsolicited emails, especially those requesting sensitive information or urgent action.
- Always verify the sender's email address. Phishing emails often come from addresses that look similar to legitimate organizations but contain subtle misspellings or unusual characters.
- Hover over links to check the actual URL before clicking. If it looks suspicious or unfamiliar, don't click.
- Use antivirus software and ensure your operating system is up-to-date to protect against malware.

16. Message App Banking Fraud

- **Modus Operandi:**

  - Fraudsters contact victims through messaging apps (like WhatsApp, SMS, or Telegram) posing as bank representatives or customer service agents. They often claim that there is an issue with the victim's bank account or that immediate action is required to prevent an account freeze.
  - The fraudster convinces the victim to share sensitive banking details, OTPs, or login credentials, claiming it's necessary to resolve the issue.
  - Once they have access to this information, fraudsters initiate unauthorized transactions or steal money from the victim's account.
  - In some cases, fraudsters may send links through messaging apps that lead to fake banking sites designed to capture the victim's login details.

- **Prevention:**

  - Banks will never ask for sensitive information (such as OTPs or passwords) via messaging apps.
  - If you receive a suspicious message claiming to be from your bank, do not respond. Instead, contact your bank directly using official channels to verify the request.
  - Never click on links received via unsolicited messages and avoid sharing any personal or financial information over messaging apps.

17. Fraudulent Loans with Stolen Documents

- **Modus Operandi:**

  - Fraudsters obtain stolen or forged personal identification documents (like passports, Aadhaar cards, or social security numbers) and use them to apply for loans in the victim's name.
  - The fraudster often works with fraudulent lending institutions or uses online loan platforms with minimal verification procedures.
  - The victim is unaware that a loan has been taken in their name until they receive notices from the lending institution demanding repayment.
  - This type of fraud not only damages the victim's credit score but also leaves them liable for repayment of a loan they never took out.

- **Prevention:**

  - Keep your personal identification documents safe

and do not share copies of them with untrusted sources.

- Monitor your credit report regularly to check for unauthorized loans or accounts opened in your name.
- If you suspect your identity has been stolen, report it immediately to law enforcement and the credit reporting agencies.

18. Betting Scam

- **Modus Operandi:**

  - Fraudsters lure victims into online betting platforms, promising quick and easy money through sports betting or gambling. These platforms often look professional and may even offer initial payouts to build trust.
  - As the victim continues to bet larger amounts, the fraudster manipulates the outcome or refuses to allow the victim to withdraw winnings.
  - In some cases, the platform disappears after a significant amount has been bet, leaving the victim unable to recover their money.
  - These scams prey on the desire for fast earnings and the excitement of betting, often leading victims to lose significant sums.

- **Prevention:**

  - Avoid unregulated or unfamiliar betting platforms. Only use reputable and licensed gambling services.
  - Be cautious of betting sites that offer guaranteed

returns or high winnings with little risk, as this is a red flag for scams.
- Read reviews and check the legitimacy of the platform before participating in online betting.
- Remember that all betting involves risk, and no outcome is guaranteed.

19. Fake Vaccination Call

- **Modus Operandi:**

  - Fraudsters call victims, posing as health officials or government representatives offering vaccination appointments or certificates. These calls became especially common during the COVID-19 pandemic.
  - The fraudster may ask for personal information, such as identification numbers, date of birth, or health insurance details, claiming it's necessary to register for the vaccine.
  - In some cases, the fraudster asks for payment to secure a vaccination slot or obtain a vaccination certificate.
  - Once the victim shares their information or makes the payment, the fraudster disappears, and no vaccine or certificate is provided.

- **Prevention:**

  - Be cautious of unsolicited calls offering vaccinations, especially if they request personal information or payment.
  - Always register for vaccinations through official government or healthcare platforms, and verify the

identity of the caller by contacting your healthcare provider directly.

- Do not provide sensitive personal details or make payments over the phone for vaccination services.

20. COVID Testing - Fake Online Site

- **Modus Operandi:**

  - Fraudsters create fake websites that appear to offer COVID-19 testing services, either at home or at testing centers. These websites often look professional and may use branding from legitimate healthcare organizations.
  - Victims are asked to pay upfront for the testing service or provide personal details to book an appointment.
  - Once the payment is made or the information is provided, the fraudster disappears, and no testing is conducted.
  - In some cases, the fraudster uses the victim's personal information for identity theft or other fraudulent activities.

- **Prevention:**

  - Always book COVID-19 tests through official healthcare providers or government-approved platforms.
  - Be cautious of online testing services that request payment upfront or ask for excessive personal details.
  - Verify the legitimacy of the testing site by checking

for official approval or accreditation from recognized healthcare authorities.

21. Fraudsters in the Pretext of Recovery Agents

- **Modus Operandi:**

  - Fraudsters pose as loan recovery agents or debt collectors for banks or financial institutions, claiming that the victim has overdue loan payments or credit card debt that must be paid immediately.
  - They use high-pressure tactics, including threats of legal action, damage to the victim's credit score, or even arrest, to coerce the victim into paying.
  - The fraudsters may ask for payments to be made to their personal account, promising to settle the debt on the victim's behalf. Once the payment is made, they disappear, and the debt remains unpaid.
  - In some cases, fraudsters may have access to basic details about the victim's financial history, making their claims appear more credible.

- **Prevention:**

  - Verify the identity of any debt collector by contacting your bank or financial institution directly. Do not make payments to any individual account without confirming its legitimacy.
  - Be wary of any unexpected or aggressive calls demanding immediate payments. Reputable debt collection agencies will provide documentation.
  - Never share sensitive financial information (such as your account details or payment information) over

the phone without verifying the caller's identity.

22. Social Welfare Scheme Fraud

- **Modus Operandi:**

  - Fraudsters impersonate government officials or agencies offering benefits under social welfare schemes, such as unemployment assistance, pensions, or healthcare services.
  - Victims are asked to provide personal information, such as their Aadhaar number, social security number, or bank account details, to apply for the benefits.
  - The fraudster may also ask for an upfront payment or processing fee to complete the application. Once the money is paid or the information is provided, the fraudster disappears.
  - Victims are left without the promised benefits and often face the risk of identity theft as their personal information is misused.

- **Prevention:**

  - Always apply for government welfare schemes through official channels, such as government websites or authorized service centers.
  - Be cautious of unsolicited calls or messages offering benefits, especially if they request personal information or payments upfront.
  - Verify the identity of any person claiming to represent a government agency by contacting the agency directly.

23. Multi-Level Marketing (MLM) Scams

- **Modus Operandi:**

  - Fraudsters recruit victims into pyramid schemes under the guise of a **Multi-Level Marketing (MLM)** opportunity. They promise high earnings by selling products or recruiting others into the scheme.
  - The scam often requires the victim to pay an upfront fee for a starter kit or inventory, which is supposed to help them sell products. However, the real focus of the scam is on recruiting more people rather than selling legitimate products.
  - As the pyramid grows, the victim is encouraged to recruit others to join, often at the cost of more upfront fees. Eventually, the scheme collapses when new recruits stop joining, leaving the victim with losses.
  - Many MLM scams offer little to no real product value, and most of the money is made through recruiting new members rather than actual sales.

- **Prevention:**

  - Be skeptical of any business opportunity that emphasizes recruiting others to make money rather than selling products.
  - Avoid schemes that require large upfront investments or ongoing purchases of inventory with the promise of guaranteed returns.
  - Research the company thoroughly, and check if it is registered with consumer protection agencies or has been flagged for fraudulent practices.

24. Work from Home Scam

- **Modus Operandi:**

  - Fraudsters post fake work-from-home job offers on job portals or social media platforms, often promising high pay for minimal work. Jobs like data entry, assembling products, or reviewing websites are commonly offered.
  - Victims are required to pay upfront fees for training, registration, or supplies before they can start the job.
  - After the payment is made, the fraudster disappears, or the "work" given is either impossible to complete or worthless. Victims are left without the promised earnings.
  - Some scams involve fake companies that collect personal information during the application process, leading to potential identity theft.

- **Prevention:**

  - Be cautious of job offers that promise high pay for little effort, especially those that require upfront fees for training or supplies.
  - Research the company offering the job and check for reviews or complaints from other job seekers.
  - Legitimate employers do not ask for registration fees, and work-from-home opportunities should not involve large financial risks.

25. Online Shopping Fraud

- **Modus Operandi:**

- ◦ Fraudsters create fake online shopping websites or post fake listings on legitimate platforms. They offer goods at significantly reduced prices to lure victims into making purchases.
- ◦ Once the victim makes the payment, the product is either never delivered or is of inferior quality compared to what was advertised.
- ◦ In some cases, fraudsters use the victim's payment details for further unauthorized transactions or sell counterfeit products under the guise of luxury or branded goods.
- ◦ Victims often have no recourse, as the fake website or seller disappears once the payment is made.

- **Prevention:**

- ◦ Shop only on reputable and well-known e-commerce platforms. Avoid websites that offer unrealistically low prices or have limited customer reviews.
- ◦ Use secure payment methods that offer buyer protection, such as credit cards or trusted payment gateways, rather than direct bank transfers or prepaid cards.
- ◦ Check the website's security features, such as "https" in the URL, and look for customer feedback or ratings before making a purchase.

26. Fraud using Public Wi-Fi

- **Modus Operandi:**

- ◦ Fraudsters set up fake public Wi-Fi networks in public places such as airports, cafes, or hotels. These networks often appear legitimate but are designed to intercept the victim's data.

- When the victim connects to the unsecured Wi-Fi, the fraudster gains access to sensitive information such as login credentials, email accounts, or payment details transmitted over the network.
- In some cases, fraudsters may use **man-in-the-middle** attacks to intercept communications between the victim and legitimate websites, allowing them to steal personal information without the victim's knowledge.

- **Prevention**:

  - Avoid using public Wi-Fi for sensitive activities, such as online banking, shopping, or accessing personal accounts.
  - Use a virtual private network (VPN) when connecting to public Wi-Fi to encrypt your data and protect it from interception.
  - Be cautious of unsecured Wi-Fi networks and only connect to Wi-Fi that you know is legitimate and secure.

27. Fake Advertisements/Offers

- **Modus Operandi**:

  - Fraudsters create fake advertisements or pop-up offers online, promising unbelievable discounts, free products, or rewards for completing simple tasks.
  - Victims are lured into clicking on these ads, which often lead to fraudulent websites designed to capture

their personal and payment information.

- In other cases, victims are asked to pay a small fee to claim a reward or enter a contest, only to realize later that the offer was fake and their money or details have been stolen.

- **Prevention**:

  - Be skeptical of advertisements or offers that seem too good to be true, especially those offering high-value items for free or at extremely low prices.
  - Avoid clicking on pop-up ads or suspicious banners, especially if they direct you to unfamiliar websites.
  - Use trusted ad blockers to reduce the risk of interacting with malicious ads.

28. Fake Loan Offer

- **Modus Operandi**:

  - Fraudsters offer loans at attractive interest rates through online advertisements, emails, or social media. They often promise easy approval with minimal paperwork, regardless of the victim's credit score.
  - To process the loan, the fraudster asks for upfront fees, such as processing fees, service charges, or insurance costs. Once the victim pays the fee, the fraudster disappears, and no loan is granted.
  - In some cases, fraudsters may also collect sensitive personal information like bank account details or identification documents for identity theft or further fraud.

- **Prevention:**

  - Be cautious of unsolicited loan offers, especially those that promise guaranteed approval or require upfront payments.
  - Verify the legitimacy of the lender by checking for proper licensing and accreditation with relevant regulatory bodies.
  - Never provide personal information or pay fees before receiving confirmation of the loan approval from a trusted source.

29. Credit Card Activation Fraud

- **Modus Operandi:**

  - Victims receive a phone call, email, or message claiming to be from their credit card provider, asking them to activate their new or existing card by providing sensitive information like the card number, CVV, or OTP.
  - The fraudster may claim that the activation is required for security purposes or to unlock special offers and benefits.
  - Once the victim shares the details, the fraudster uses the information to make unauthorized transactions or withdraw money from the victim's account.

- **Prevention:**

  - Banks and credit card companies do not ask for sensitive information like CVV or OTPs to activate credit cards. Activation is typically done through official channels, such as secure websites or verified phone numbers.

○ Never share credit card details, CVV, or OTP with unsolicited callers or messages.

○ If you receive such a request, contact your bank directly using the customer service number on the back of your card to verify the claim.

30. Credit Card Limit Upgradation Fraud

- **Modus Operandi:**

  ○ Fraudsters contact the victim, posing as representatives from the bank, offering to increase the credit limit on their card. They may offer attractive incentives such as lower interest rates or exclusive benefits.

  ○ To process the limit increase, the fraudster asks for credit card details, OTPs, or personal identification information under the guise of verifying the cardholder's identity.

  ○ Once the victim shares this information, the fraudster uses it to carry out unauthorized transactions or withdraw money from the victim's account.

- **Prevention:**

  ○ Be cautious of unsolicited offers to increase your credit card limit, especially if they ask for sensitive details like CVV or OTP.

  ○ Verify any such offers by contacting your bank directly through official customer service channels.

- Legitimate credit card limit increases do not require you to share personal information over the phone or email.

31. Safeguarding your Aadhaar Card

- **Modus Operandi:**

  - Fraudsters misuse Aadhaar card details to commit identity theft and fraud. They may acquire copies of Aadhaar cards through phishing emails, fake job offers, or fake government schemes.
  - With the Aadhaar details, fraudsters can open bank accounts, apply for loans, or commit other fraudulent financial activities in the victim's name.
  - Sometimes, fraudsters trick victims into sharing Aadhaar details, claiming they are necessary for KYC (Know Your Customer) updates or government schemes.

- **Prevention:**

  - Never share your Aadhaar number or a copy of your Aadhaar card with untrusted sources. Be cautious when submitting your Aadhaar details online.
  - Use the **Aadhaar Virtual ID (VID)** when asked for Aadhaar verification. This temporary code can be used instead of the actual Aadhaar number to protect your information.
  - Regularly monitor your bank accounts and credit report for unauthorized activities and report any suspicious actions to the authorities.

32. Online Fraud using Cashback Offers

- **Modus Operandi:**

  - Fraudsters create fake cashback offers, often through email, social media, or fake websites, promising substantial cashback on purchases made using specific links or promo codes.
  - Victims are lured by the offer and either share sensitive details like bank account information or make purchases through fraudulent websites.
  - In some cases, victims are asked to make upfront payments to claim the cashback or are tricked into clicking malicious links that steal their personal and financial details.

- **Prevention:**

  - Be cautious of unsolicited offers of cashback or discounts from unknown sources, especially if they ask for personal or financial details.
  - Only use cashback offers from trusted platforms or well-known e-commerce sites. Verify the legitimacy of the offer through official sources.
  - Avoid clicking on suspicious links in emails or social media messages, especially those that require you to share sensitive information.

33. Discount Fraud

- **Modus Operandi:**

  - Fraudsters offer unrealistic discounts on popular

products or services through fake websites, social media, or pop-up ads. These discounts often appear too good to be true, luring victims into making quick purchases.

- Victims make payments but never receive the goods, or they receive counterfeit or low-quality products. The fraudsters disappear after receiving the payment.
- In some cases, fraudsters use the victim's payment details to commit further unauthorized transactions.

- **Prevention:**

  - Always verify the legitimacy of discounts, especially if the offer seems unusually generous. Research the seller and read customer reviews before making any purchase.
  - Shop from well-established e-commerce platforms and avoid making purchases from unfamiliar websites.
  - Use secure payment methods that offer protection, such as credit cards or trusted payment gateways.

34. Charity Frauds

- **Modus Operandi:**

  - Fraudsters create fake charities, often during times of crisis (e.g., natural disasters or pandemics), and solicit donations from unsuspecting victims.
  - Victims, believing they are donating to a worthy cause, transfer money to the fraudster's account. The fraudster may use official-sounding names or mimic

legitimate charities to gain trust.

- In addition to stealing donations, fraudsters may also collect personal details that can be used for identity theft.

- **Prevention:**

  - Always donate to well-known, reputable charities. Verify the legitimacy of the charity through trusted sources like official websites or charity accreditation agencies.
  - Be cautious of unsolicited requests for donations, especially through social media or email.
  - Avoid sharing personal information or making donations to individuals or organizations that do not provide transparent information about their activities.

35. Overdraft Against FD (Fixed Deposit)

- **Modus Operandi:**

  - Fraudsters use stolen or forged documents related to the victim's Fixed Deposit (FD) account to take out loans or overdrafts against the FD without the victim's knowledge.
  - In some cases, insiders at financial institutions may collude with fraudsters to access the victim's FD details and misuse them to secure loans.
  - The victim remains unaware of the loan until they receive notices for repayment or until their FD matures and they find that the funds have been withdrawn.

- **Prevention:**

  - Regularly monitor your FD accounts and ensure that you receive all communication related to your FD from the bank.
  - Avoid sharing sensitive details of your FD accounts, especially with unauthorized individuals.
  - Set up alerts with your bank to notify you of any changes or transactions related to your FD.

36. Frauds using Malicious Applications

- **Modus Operandi:**

  - Fraudsters trick victims into downloading malicious applications that appear to be legitimate tools or services, such as banking apps, games, or utility apps.
  - Once installed, these apps gain access to sensitive information on the victim's device, such as login credentials, personal data, and banking details. Some malicious apps can even control the victim's device remotely or track their keystrokes (keylogging).
  - Victims may unknowingly grant permissions to these apps, allowing the fraudsters to carry out unauthorized transactions, steal data, or monitor their activities.

- **Prevention:**

  - Download apps only from trusted sources, such as the official Google Play Store or Apple App Store, and avoid installing apps from third-party websites.
  - Read app reviews and check the developer's

information before downloading.

- Monitor app permissions closely and avoid granting unnecessary permissions to apps that request access to sensitive information.

37. Illegal Loan Financing Apps with Exorbitant Interest Rates and Harassment Tactics

- **Modus Operandi:**

  - Fraudsters create illegal loan apps that offer easy access to quick loans with minimal verification. However, these loans come with hidden terms, such as exorbitant interest rates and harsh repayment conditions.
  - Victims, often in need of quick cash, take out the loan without realizing the actual cost. When they are unable to repay on time, the fraudsters use aggressive collection methods, including threats, harassment, and shaming.
  - In some cases, fraudsters also misuse the victim's personal contacts (accessed via the app) to publicly humiliate or harass the borrower.

- **Prevention:**

  - Only borrow from licensed and regulated financial institutions. Verify the legitimacy of loan apps before downloading and using them.
  - Read the terms and conditions carefully, especially with regard to interest rates, repayment schedules, and penalties for late payment.
  - Report illegal loan apps to relevant authorities and

seek legal assistance if you are being harassed.

38. Card Cloning at Merchant Outlets

- **Modus Operandi:**

  - Fraudsters install skimming devices on card machines at merchant outlets, restaurants, or petrol stations. These devices capture the data from the magnetic stripe of the victim's card when it is swiped or inserted.
  - The fraudster then creates a cloned card with the stolen data, which they use to make unauthorized purchases or withdraw money from the victim's account.
  - Victims often only discover the fraud after reviewing their bank statements or noticing unauthorized transactions.

- **Prevention:**

  - Avoid using your card in unfamiliar or suspicious merchant outlets. Opt for chip-based transactions, as chip cards are more secure than magnetic stripe cards.
  - Monitor your bank account regularly for unauthorized transactions and report any suspicious activity to your bank immediately.
  - Cover the keypad when entering your PIN at any card terminal to prevent fraudsters from capturing it.

39. Fraud through Details Shared with Known Person/Family/Relatives

- **Modus Operandi:**

  - In this type of fraud, victims unknowingly share sensitive financial details (such as card numbers, passwords, or bank account information) with trusted family members, friends, or relatives who then misuse the information.
  - The fraudster, who may be a close acquaintance, uses the victim's trust to access their accounts or make unauthorized transactions without the victim's knowledge.
  - The victim often only realizes the fraud after seeing unauthorized charges or withdrawals from their account.

- **Prevention:**

  - Be cautious about sharing sensitive financial details, even with trusted family members or friends. Always maintain privacy around your banking information.
  - Regularly monitor your accounts for any unauthorized activity.
  - Consider using strong passwords and two-factor authentication (2FA) to secure your financial accounts.

40. Payment Spoofing Applications

- **Modus Operandi:**

  - Fraudsters use fake payment apps to show false payment confirmations. These apps are designed to mimic legitimate payment apps and display a fake "successful transaction" screen.

- The fraudster may show the victim this screen to convince them that the payment has been made, while in reality, no money has been transferred.
- This type of fraud is common in peer-to-peer transactions, such as when selling items on online marketplaces or through personal sales.

- **Prevention:**

  - Always verify payment by checking your bank account or digital wallet directly to ensure the transaction has been credited.
  - Avoid relying on screenshots or transaction confirmation pages, as these can be faked.
  - Use trusted and secure payment platforms that provide real-time notifications for transactions.

41. Sextortion

- **Modus Operandi:**

  - **Sextortion** is a form of cybercrime where fraudsters coerce victims into performing sexual acts or sharing explicit images or videos, often through manipulation or threats.
  - It typically begins with the fraudster gaining the victim's trust through social media, dating apps, or online chat platforms. They may initiate a romantic or friendly conversation, building rapport over time.
  - Once trust is established, the fraudster convinces the victim to share explicit content, either through photos, videos, or video calls.

- After obtaining compromising material, the fraudster threatens to publicly share the explicit content with the victim's friends, family, or colleagues unless a ransom is paid. This payment is often demanded in cryptocurrency to make it harder to trace.
- Victims may also be blackmailed into providing more explicit content in exchange for the fraudster not releasing the material.

- **Prevention**:

  - Avoid sharing explicit images or videos online or with individuals you do not know personally. Even with trusted individuals, be cautious about sharing sensitive content.
  - Be aware of the privacy risks on social media and dating platforms. Fraudsters often create fake profiles to target potential victims.
  - If you are threatened with sextortion, do not comply with the demands. Report the crime to law enforcement authorities and cease all contact with the fraudster.
  - Use strong privacy settings on social media and limit the amount of personal information you share online.

42. WhatsApp Video Call Fraud

- **Modus Operandi**:

  - In **WhatsApp Video Call Fraud**, fraudsters initiate a video call through WhatsApp, often posing as someone familiar to the victim or a potential romantic interest.

- During the call, the fraudster manipulates or tricks the victim into doing something compromising, such as undressing or engaging in inappropriate behavior.
- The fraudster secretly records the call and later threatens to share the video with the victim's contacts or post it on social media unless a ransom is paid, usually in cryptocurrency or via direct transfer.
- The fraudster may also edit the video to make it appear more compromising than it is and increase the pressure on the victim to pay.
- Sometimes, fraudsters use fake profiles or deepfake technology to impersonate celebrities or well-known figures, making the scam seem more believable to the victim.

- **Prevention:**

  - Be cautious when accepting video calls from unknown or suspicious contacts, especially if they initiate the call unexpectedly.
  - Do not engage in any compromising activity during video calls with people you do not know well or trust. Assume that any video call could be recorded.
  - If you receive a threatening message after a video call, do not panic or make any payments. Block the contact and report the incident to WhatsApp and local law enforcement.
  - Strengthen your privacy settings on WhatsApp, including restricting who can see your profile photo, status, and contact information.

43. Digital Arrest

- **Modus Operandi:**

  - **Digital Arrest** scams involve fraudsters pretending to be law enforcement officers, government agents, or legal authorities. They contact the victim, claiming that the victim has committed a crime (often related to financial fraud, illegal activities, or a data breach) and that they are under "digital arrest."
  - The fraudster claims that the victim must pay a fine, provide personal information, or transfer funds to avoid legal action, jail time, or a court trial. These fines are often requested in the form of cryptocurrency, prepaid cards, or direct transfers to untraceable accounts.
  - Fraudsters often use intimidation tactics, such as fake arrest warrants, official-looking documents, or threats of immediate arrest, to coerce victims into paying.
  - In some cases, they may impersonate cybersecurity experts, claiming that the victim's computer or accounts have been compromised and offering to help "fix" the issue for a fee.

- **Prevention:**

  - Be skeptical of unsolicited calls or messages claiming to be from law enforcement or government agencies, especially if they demand immediate payment or personal information.
  - Law enforcement agencies will never ask for fines or payments through unconventional methods like

cryptocurrency or prepaid cards.

- Do not share sensitive information such as passwords, financial data, or personal identification numbers over the phone or email, especially with unverified sources.
- If you receive a suspicious message or call, contact the relevant government agency or law enforcement department directly using official contact details to verify the claim.

44. Task Fraud

- **Modus Operandi:**

  - In **Task Fraud**, fraudsters lure victims into completing simple online tasks, such as liking videos, sharing social media posts, or filling out surveys, often in exchange for small payments.
  - Initially, the fraudster pays small amounts to gain the victim's trust, making it appear as though they are earning money easily.
  - As the tasks progress, the fraudster asks for larger sums of money under the pretext of unlocking higher-paying tasks, gaining access to more profitable opportunities, or paying for a registration fee.
  - Once the victim pays, the fraudster vanishes, or they continue asking for more money under various excuses. No substantial payment or reward is ever given to the victim.
  - Victims lose both the money they've paid upfront and any time they've invested in completing the tasks.

- **Prevention:**

  - Be cautious of any offers that promise easy money for completing simple tasks, especially if they require upfront payments.
  - Avoid any job or task offers that require you to pay fees in advance or make deposits to unlock higher-paying work.
  - Always research platforms offering such tasks or rewards before participating. Check for reviews and feedback from other users to verify legitimacy.
  - If an opportunity seems too good to be true, it likely is.

45. Fake Share Trading

- **Modus Operandi:**

  - Fraudsters create fake online trading platforms or apps that mimic legitimate stock trading services. These platforms offer shares of well-known companies or invite victims to invest in "hot" stocks that promise high returns in a short time.
  - Victims are encouraged to open trading accounts, invest in stocks, and are often shown fake returns in their portfolios to lure them into investing more.
  - The fraudster may also promise insider tips or guaranteed profits. Once the victim invests a significant amount, the fraudster either blocks access to the account, shows losses in fake stock trades, or disappears entirely.
  - In some cases, victims are asked to pay additional fees to withdraw their funds or are convinced to

invest even more to recover their losses.
- Ultimately, the victim loses their initial investment and any additional funds they've put into the platform.

- **Prevention**:

  - Be cautious of any trading platform or app that guarantees high returns or promises insider tips. Legitimate trading platforms do not offer guaranteed profits.
  - Always verify that the trading platform is registered with the relevant financial regulatory authority in your country.
  - Use well-established, trusted brokerage firms for stock trading and investments.
  - Avoid making payments or deposits into unregulated platforms, especially if they request payments through unconventional methods like cryptocurrency or prepaid cards.

46. Fake Crypto Trading

- **Modus Operandi**:

  - Fraudsters set up fake cryptocurrency exchanges, trading platforms, or investment schemes that promise quick and massive returns by trading or investing in popular cryptocurrencies like **Bitcoin**, **Ethereum**, or new and obscure tokens.
  - Victims are enticed by promises of low-risk, high-reward investments. They are often given initial payouts or shown fake gains in their accounts to

build trust and encourage them to invest more.

- ○ Once the victim has invested a substantial amount, the fraudster either blocks access to the platform or invents reasons why the funds cannot be withdrawn (such as the need to pay taxes, additional fees, or other costs).
- ○ In some cases, fraudsters may simply disappear with the victim's funds, and the fake platform is shut down, leaving victims with no way to recover their money.
- ○ Fraudsters may also use phishing techniques to steal cryptocurrency wallet credentials or private keys, allowing them to steal the victim's cryptocurrency holdings directly.

- **Prevention**:

- ○ Be wary of any cryptocurrency platform that promises guaranteed profits or offers unusually high returns with little to no risk.
- ○ Use only well-established, regulated cryptocurrency exchanges and wallets for buying, selling, and trading digital assets.
- ○ Avoid platforms that require you to deposit funds before you can withdraw earnings or that ask for additional payments for "unlocking" funds.
- ○ Secure your cryptocurrency wallet with strong security practices, such as using two-factor authentication (2FA) and never sharing your private keys or seed phrases.

47. Fake Antivirus/Tech Support Scams

- **Modus Operandi:**

  - Fraudsters pose as tech support agents or antivirus providers, contacting victims via phone, email, or pop-up messages that claim the victim's computer has been infected with malware.
  - They offer to "fix" the problem if the victim grants remote access to their computer or pays a fee for fake antivirus software.
  - Once they gain access to the victim's computer, they may steal personal data, install malware, or extort more money for additional services.

- **Prevention:**

  - Do not respond to unsolicited tech support calls or pop-up messages claiming your computer is infected.
  - Use legitimate antivirus software and download it only from trusted sources.
  - If you suspect your computer has been compromised, contact a trusted tech support provider directly.

48. Bait-and-Switch Fraud

- **Modus Operandi:**

  - Fraudsters advertise a product or service at an attractively low price to lure victims into making a purchase. However, when the victim tries to buy the product, they are either upsold a more expensive item or are given a substandard product that is different from what was advertised.

- The fraudster often pressures the victim to accept the inferior product, claiming it is of equal or higher value, or they use excuses to avoid delivering the original item.

- **Prevention**:

  - Be cautious of advertisements offering products at unusually low prices.
  - Research the seller and product before making any purchase.
  - If the product you receive is different from what was advertised, report the issue immediately and request a refund or replacement.

49. Imposter Scams

- **Modus Operandi**:

  - In imposter scams, fraudsters pose as trusted individuals, such as family members, government officials, or company executives. They contact the victim with an urgent request, often asking for money, personal information, or assistance with a task.
  - Common variations include scammers pretending to be a grandchild needing emergency funds, a government official asking for taxes, or a CEO requesting gift cards for employees.
  - The victim, believing the imposter's claim, sends money or provides information, only to realize later that the request was fake.

- **Prevention**:

  - Always verify the identity of anyone asking for money or sensitive information, even if they claim to be someone you know or trust.
  - If someone contacts you claiming to be a family member in distress, reach out to them through another channel to confirm the request.
  - Be cautious of requests for unusual payment methods, such as gift cards, wire transfers, or cryptocurrency.

50. Illegal Item in Courier Scam

- **Modus Operandi**:

  - In the **Illegal Item in Courier Scam**, fraudsters impersonate representatives from reputable courier companies to trick victims into sharing sensitive information or transferring money. The scam typically begins with the victim receiving a phone call or email from someone claiming to be from FedEx, informing them that a package in their name contains **illegal substances** (such as drugs or contraband) or other suspicious items.
  - The fraudster creates a sense of urgency by claiming that the police or customs authorities are involved, and the victim needs to cooperate to avoid legal action, including **arrest** or **fines**. To "verify" the identity or process the issue, the fraudster asks the victim to provide **personal information** such as bank account details, internet banking credentials, credit card information, or **One-Time Passwords (OTPs)**.

- ○ In some variations of the scam, the fraudster may direct the victim to transfer funds to another account under the pretense of resolving the issue. They may claim that the victim must pay **customs fees, legal fines**, or **"unfreeze" the account** associated with the illegal package. Once the victim transfers the funds or provides their banking details, the fraudster steals the money or uses the information to apply for loans or make unauthorized transactions.

- **Prevention:**

- **Verify all claims**: If you receive a call or email from someone claiming to be from FedEx or any other courier company, verify the legitimacy of the communication by contacting the courier directly using official contact information found on their website. Do not rely on contact details provided by the caller or email.
- **Never share personal or banking information**: Legitimate companies will never ask for personal details like bank account numbers, credit card information, or OTPs over the phone or email. Avoid sharing sensitive information with anyone claiming to represent a courier service or law enforcement.
- **Beware of urgency tactics**: Fraudsters often use fear and urgency to pressure victims into quick decisions. If you receive a message that feels threatening or too urgent, take a step back and verify the situation before taking any action.
- **Do not transfer money based on phone calls**: Never transfer money to a third party based on claims about a suspicious package, legal trouble, or courier-related

issues. Always verify such requests independently.

- **Report the scam**: If you suspect you are being targeted by a Illegal Item in Courier Scam or any similar fraud, report the incident to your local **cybercrime helpline** or law enforcement authorities immediately.

Resources For Reporting Cyber Crimes

Reporting Cyber Crimes in India

1. **National Cyber Crime Reporting Portal:**

   - **Website:** cybercrime.gov.in – A central platform to report cyber crimes and online frauds.

2. **Local Police Stations:**

   - File a complaint at your local police station, where dedicated cyber crime cells handle such issues.

3. **State Cyber Crime Cells:**

   - Check your state's police department website for contact details and reporting procedures specific to your state.

4. **National Computer Emergency Response Team (CERT-IN):**

   - **Website:** cert-in.org.in – Provides guidance and assistance for severe cyber incidents.

5. **Cyber Crime Investigation Cell:**

   - Part of various state police departments, these cells handle significant cyber crimes. Check your state police website for more information.

6. **Consumer Protection Websites:**

   ○ **National Consumer Helpline:** consumerhelpline.gov.in – Report online frauds related to consumer issues.

7. **Banking Ombudsman:**

   ○ Report banking fraud to the Banking Ombudsman of the respective bank or financial institution involved.

8. **Cyber Crime Awareness Portals:**

   ○ **Cyber Aware:** cyberaware.gov.in – Offers resources and tools for reporting cyber safety and crimes.

Reporting Abuse on Social Media Platforms

1. **Facebook:**

   ○ **Via Desktop:**

     ▪ Go to the profile or page with the abuse.
     ▪ Click on the three dots (•••) next to the post, comment, or message.
     ▪ Select "**Find Support or Report Post**" and follow the prompts.

   ○ **Via Mobile App:**

     ▪ Tap the three dots (•••) on the post or comment.
     ▪ Choose "**Report**" and follow the instructions.

2. **Twitter:**

   - **Via Desktop:**

     - Click the down arrow (▼) on the tweet.
     - Select **"Report Tweet"** and follow the prompts.

   - **Via Mobile App:**

     - Tap the down arrow (▼) on the tweet.
     - Choose **"Report Tweet"** and complete the report process.

3. **Instagram:**

   - **Via Desktop:**

     - Go to the profile or post with the abuse.
     - Click the three dots (•••) next to the post or profile.
     - Select **"Report"** and follow the steps.

   - **Via Mobile App:**

     - Tap the three dots (•••) next to the post or profile.
     - Choose **"Report"** and follow the prompts.

4. **LinkedIn:**

   - **Via Desktop:**

     - Go to the post or profile with the abuse.

- Click the three dots (•••) on the post or profile.
- Select "**Report**" and follow the instructions.

- **Via Mobile App:**

  - Tap the three dots (•••) next to the post or on a profile.
  - Choose "**Report**" and follow the prompts.

5. **YouTube:**

- **Via Desktop:**

  - Click on the three dots (•••) next to the video.
  - Select "**Report**" and choose the reason for reporting.

- **Via Mobile App:**

  - Tap the three dots (•••) under the video.
  - Choose "**Report**" and follow the prompts

Glossary Of Terms

- **Aadhaar Data Breach**: A significant cyber incident in India where sensitive personal information linked to the Aadhaar system was allegedly compromised.
- **Adware**: Software that automatically displays or downloads advertising material when a user is online, often bundled with free applications.
- **Advanced Persistent Threat (APT)**: A prolonged and targeted cyber attack in which an intruder gains access to a network and remains undetected for an extended period to steal data or cause damage.
- **Bait-and-Switch Fraud**: A deceptive practice where fraudsters advertise a product or service at a low price to lure victims but then sell a different, often inferior product.
- **Baiting**: A social engineering attack that entices victims with something appealing (such as free goods or services) to gain access to sensitive information.
- **BharatNet Project**: An Indian government initiative aimed at providing high-speed broadband connectivity to rural areas across India.
- **Big Data**: Large volumes of data that cannot be processed effectively with traditional data management tools, often used to train AI models.
- **Bitcoin**: A decentralized cryptocurrency used in financial transactions and often favored by cybercriminals due to its anonymity.
- **Botnet**: A network of compromised computers (bots) controlled by an attacker to perform coordinated attacks, such as sending spam emails or launching

Distributed Denial of Service (DDoS) attacks.

- **Brute Force Attack**: A trial-and-error method used to decode encrypted data such as passwords by trying all possible combinations.
- **Card Cloning at Merchant Outlets**: A method where fraudsters install skimming devices at merchant outlets to capture card information and clone cards.
- **CERT-In (Indian Computer Emergency Response Team)**: The national agency responsible for responding to cybersecurity incidents, providing technical assistance, and mitigating threats in India.
- **Charity Frauds**: Scams where fake charities are created to solicit donations from unsuspecting victims, especially during times of crisis.
- **Cloud Computing**: The delivery of computing services over the internet, often utilized for storage, processing, and software delivery, which presents unique cybersecurity challenges.
- **Cosmos Bank Cyber Heist**: A major cyber theft incident in 2018 where hackers siphoned ₹94 crore from Pune-based Cosmos Bank through a combination of ATM and SWIFT-related attacks.
- **Cyber Extortion**: Criminal activities where cybercriminals threaten harm unless their demands, typically for ransom, are met.
- **Cyber Forensics**: The practice of collecting, preserving, and analyzing digital evidence from cybercrime incidents to solve cases and support legal proceedings.
- **Cyber Stalking**: The use of electronic communications to harass or stalk individuals, often involving threats, and invasion of privacy.
- **Cyber Terrorism**: The use of digital tools to carry out attacks against a nation's infrastructure, aiming to cause

damage or fear.

- **Cyber Theft**: The unauthorized taking of information or digital assets, which can lead to significant financial and personal losses.
- **Dark Web**: A part of the internet not indexed by search engines, often associated with illegal activities such as the sale of drugs, weapons, and stolen data.
- **Data Breach**: An incident where confidential, sensitive, or protected data is accessed, used, or disclosed by an unauthorized individual.
- **Data Localization**: A legal requirement mandating that data about a nation's residents be collected, processed, and stored within that country.
- **Denial of Service (DoS) Attack**: A cyber attack that floods a network, server, or service with excessive requests, making it unavailable to legitimate users.
- **DNS Spoofing**: A type of cyber attack where a hacker corrupts the DNS server, redirecting traffic from a legitimate website to a fake one designed to steal sensitive information.
- **Drive-by Download**: A type of cyber attack in which malware is automatically downloaded onto a user's device without their knowledge when they visit a compromised website.
- **DDoS (Distributed Denial of Service)**: A type of cyber attack where multiple systems flood a targeted system with traffic, overwhelming its resources and causing service disruptions.
- **Fake Crypto Trading**: Scams using bogus cryptocurrency trading platforms promising high returns, only to defraud investors of their funds.
- **Fake Share Trading**: Scams involving counterfeit trading platforms that entice victims to invest in non-

existent stocks.

- **Firewall**: A network security system that monitors and controls incoming and outgoing network traffic based on predetermined security rules.
- **Hacking**: Unauthorized access to computer systems or networks with the intent to steal, alter, or destroy data.
- **Illegal Loan Financing Apps**: Apps that lure victims with quick loans under harsh conditions and use aggressive tactics for repayment.
- **Illegal Item in Courier Scam**: A scam involving fraudsters impersonating courier services to alarm victims with false claims of illegal items in packages.
- **Imposter Scams**: Scams where fraudsters impersonate trusted individuals or entities to solicit money, personal information, or assistance in deceptive schemes.
- **Internet of Things (IoT)**: A network of interconnected devices that communicate and share data, often exploited by cybercriminals due to weak security protocols.
- **Keylogger**: A type of malware that records keystrokes on a victim's device, capturing sensitive information like passwords and credit card numbers.
- **Man-in-the-Middle (MitM) Attack**: A cyber attack where the attacker secretly intercepts and possibly alters communication between two parties who believe they are directly communicating with each other.
- **Malware**: Malicious software designed to damage, disrupt, or gain unauthorized access to computer systems.
- **Multi-Factor Authentication (MFA)**: A security process that requires multiple forms of verification to access a system or account, enhancing security by adding an extra layer beyond just passwords.

- **Overdraft Against FD (Fixed Deposit)**: A scam involving the unauthorized use of a victim's Fixed Deposit details to secure loans or overdrafts without their knowledge.
- **Payment Spoofing Applications**: Apps designed to show false payment confirmations, tricking victims into believing that a payment has been made.
- **Pegasus Spyware**: A highly sophisticated form of spyware developed by the NSO Group, used to monitor targeted individuals' phones and communications.
- **Phishing**: A form of fraud where attackers impersonate legitimate institutions via email or other digital channels to steal sensitive data like login credentials or financial information.
- **Ransomware**: A type of malware that encrypts a victim's files, demanding payment (usually in cryptocurrency) for decryption.
- **Ransomware as a Service (RaaS)**: A business model where ransomware is sold or leased to criminals who then carry out attacks, with profits shared between the developer and the operator.
- **Session Hijacking**: A type of cyber attack where an attacker takes over a session between a client and server, gaining unauthorized access to sensitive information.
- **SIM Swap Fraud**: A type of cyber fraud where an attacker convinces a telecom provider to switch the victim's phone number to a new SIM card, gaining control over their accounts and personal information.
- **Smishing**: A form of phishing that uses SMS messages to trick victims into revealing sensitive information.
- **Social Engineering**: Techniques used by cybercriminals to manipulate individuals into revealing confidential

information or performing actions that compromise security.

- **Spoofing**: Creating a fraudulent website or email that mimics a legitimate source to deceive individuals into revealing personal or financial information.
- **Spyware**: Malicious software that monitors and collects information from a user's device without their knowledge.
- **SQL Injection**: A type of cyber attack where an attacker injects malicious SQL queries into a website's database to manipulate or extract information.
- **Task Fraud**: Scams where victims are enticed to perform tasks for payment, which escalate in cost and never result in significant earnings.
- **Threat Actor**: An individual or group responsible for a cyber attack, which can include hackers, organized crime groups, or state-sponsored entities.
- **Trojan Horse**: A type of malware that disguises itself as legitimate software but performs malicious activities once installed on a user's device.
- **Two-Factor Authentication (2FA)**: An additional layer of security used to ensure that individuals trying to access an online account are who they say they are by requiring two forms of identification.
- **Virtual Private Network (VPN)**: A service that encrypts internet traffic and hides the user's IP address, providing increased privacy and security while accessing the internet.
- **Whaling**: A type of phishing attack that targets high-profile individuals within an organization, such as executives, to steal sensitive information or execute fraudulent transactions.
- **Zero-Day Exploit**: A vulnerability in software that is

unknown to the vendor and can be exploited by attackers before it is patched or fixed.

- **Zombie Computer**: A computer that has been compromised by malware and can be controlled remotely by an attacker, often used as part of a botnet for malicious activities.

www.ingramcontent.com/pod-product-compliance
Lightning Source LLC
Chambersburg PA
CBHW031049160726
47991CB00005B/2084